Q is for QUILT

by Diana McClun and Laura Nownes

Editors: Jan Grigsby, Beate Marie Nellemann
Technical Editors: Carolyn Aune, Gael Helander Betts
Copy Editor: Lee Jonsson
Cover Designer: Christina D. Jarumay
Design Director/Book Designer: Christina D. Jarumay
Illustrator: Kandy Petersen
Production Assistant: Kristy A. Konitzer
Photography: Sharon Risedorph, all quilts except as noted below. Quilts on pages 12, 14, 16, 26, 41, 48, 62, Kathleen Bellesiles
Published by C&T Publishing, Inc., P.O. Box 1456
Lafayette, California 94549
Front Cover: *Birds Return*
Back Cover: *Rebirth of the Garden*

Attention Teachers: C&T Publishing, Inc. encourages you to use this book as a text for teaching. Contact us at 1-800-284-1114 or **www.ctpub.com** for more information about the C&T Teachers Program.

Library of Congress Cataloging-in-Publication Data

McClun, Diana,
Q is for quilt / Diana McClun and Laura Nownes.
p. cm.
ISBN 1-57120-181-5 (paper trade)
1. Quilting--Patterns. 2. Patchwork--Patterns. I. Nownes, Laura, II. Title.
TT835 .M2749 2002
746.46'041--dc21

2002001803

Printed in China
10 9 8 7 6 5 4 3 2

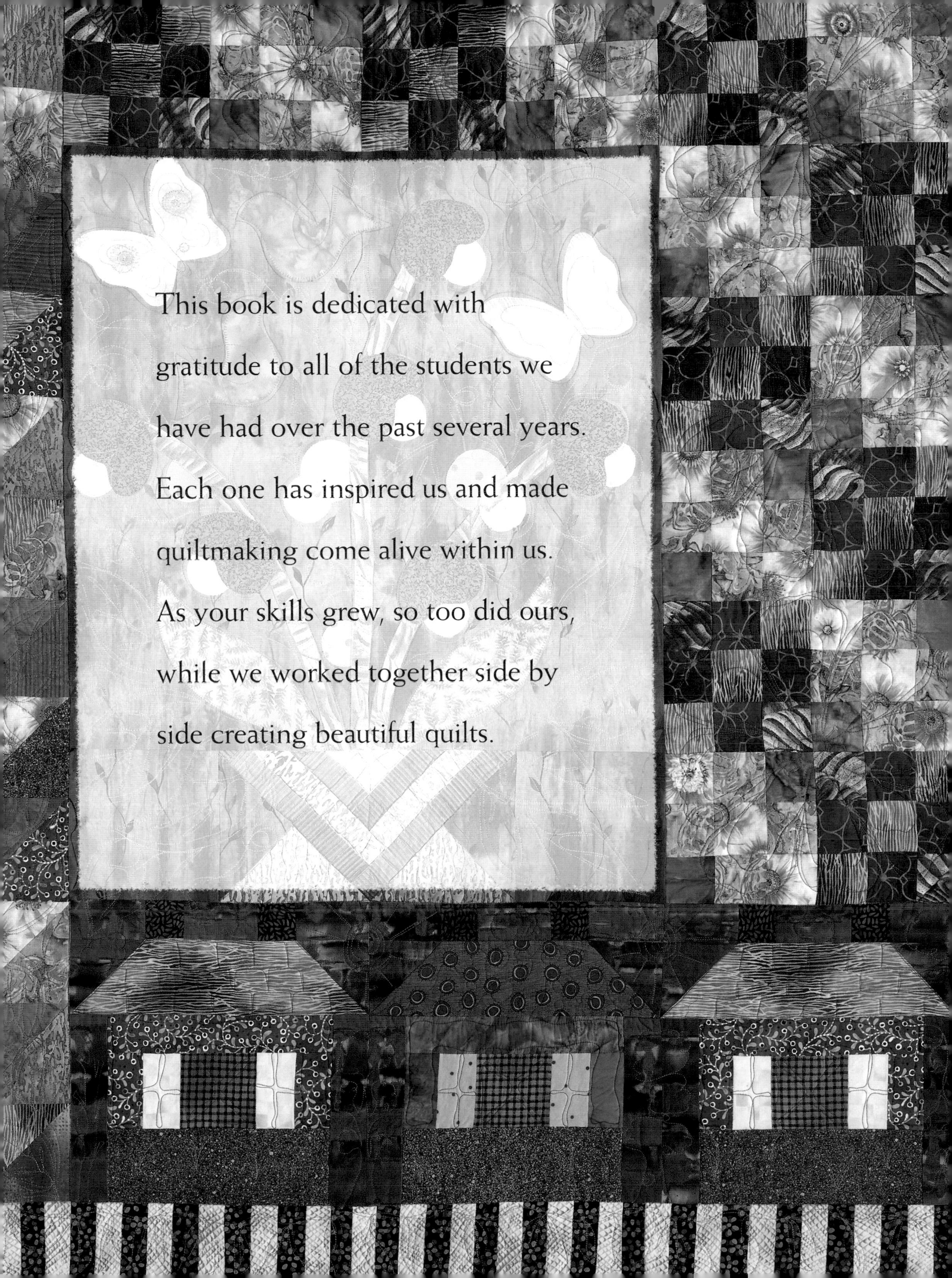

This book is dedicated with gratitude to all of the students we have had over the past several years. Each one has inspired us and made quiltmaking come alive within us. As your skills grew, so too did ours, while we worked together side by side creating beautiful quilts.

TABLE OF

CONTENTS

Introduction

Another book for our students to enjoy was a resounding theme that kept running through our heads. So we asked the questions: What does our beginning student want? What does our intermediate student want? We went to work to find the answers. We found what they wanted were simple patterns to piece and appliqué.

They wanted blocks that could be used to tell their own personal stories. They wanted blocks that would inspire and challenge their aesthetics and, at the same time, further their growth in the art of quiltmaking.

We are pleased and excited to present to you a collection of seven simple blocks that we feel meet the needs of our students. *Q is for Quilt* starts with the basic Nine-Patch block. This pattern was used in Diana's first quilt when she was seven years old. The simple Nine-Patches covered her doll's bed. It was her first sewing machine experience, and it has been preserved to keep the memories alive of her first quiltmaking experience.

Laura's first quilt was a sampler. With this in mind, we know the sampler is a good teaching format with a variety of blocks covering a range of techniques to assist in the process of mastering the basics of quiltmaking.

How to Use This Book

Q *is for Quilt* has been organized by pattern, in order of levels of difficulty in construction. Each chapter begins with specific instructions and sewing order diagrams for making the quilt block. Following that are several projects which use the block in a variety of color and setting options. Yardage and cutting charts are often included for making the quilts in several sizes. Because we prefer to have extra fabric (to add to our stash) rather than run out in the middle of a project, we have been generous with the fabric requirements. Helpful hints, notes, and checkpoints throughout the book are intended to attract your attention and assist you where needed.

We encourage you to review the desired project pattern and become familiar with the block construction and techniques to make it. General Instructions begin on page 94. Fabric suggestions are included with each project. Enjoy selecting fabrics which reflect your taste. If you are new to quiltmaking, you might first consider following the instructions for making the blocks at the beginning of each chapter. The blocks can be included in a sampler quilt following the class outline found on page 110. This will allow you to discover which patterns you may want to make into an entire quilt, as well as learn new techniques or fine tune those you are already familiar with.

The gallery includes several quilts that were made by our students. They were given the patterns and encouraged to play with color and setting options. We invite you to do the same and hope you will be inspired, too—while furthering your growth and enjoyment in the art of quiltmaking.

CHAPTER 1

The Starting Point

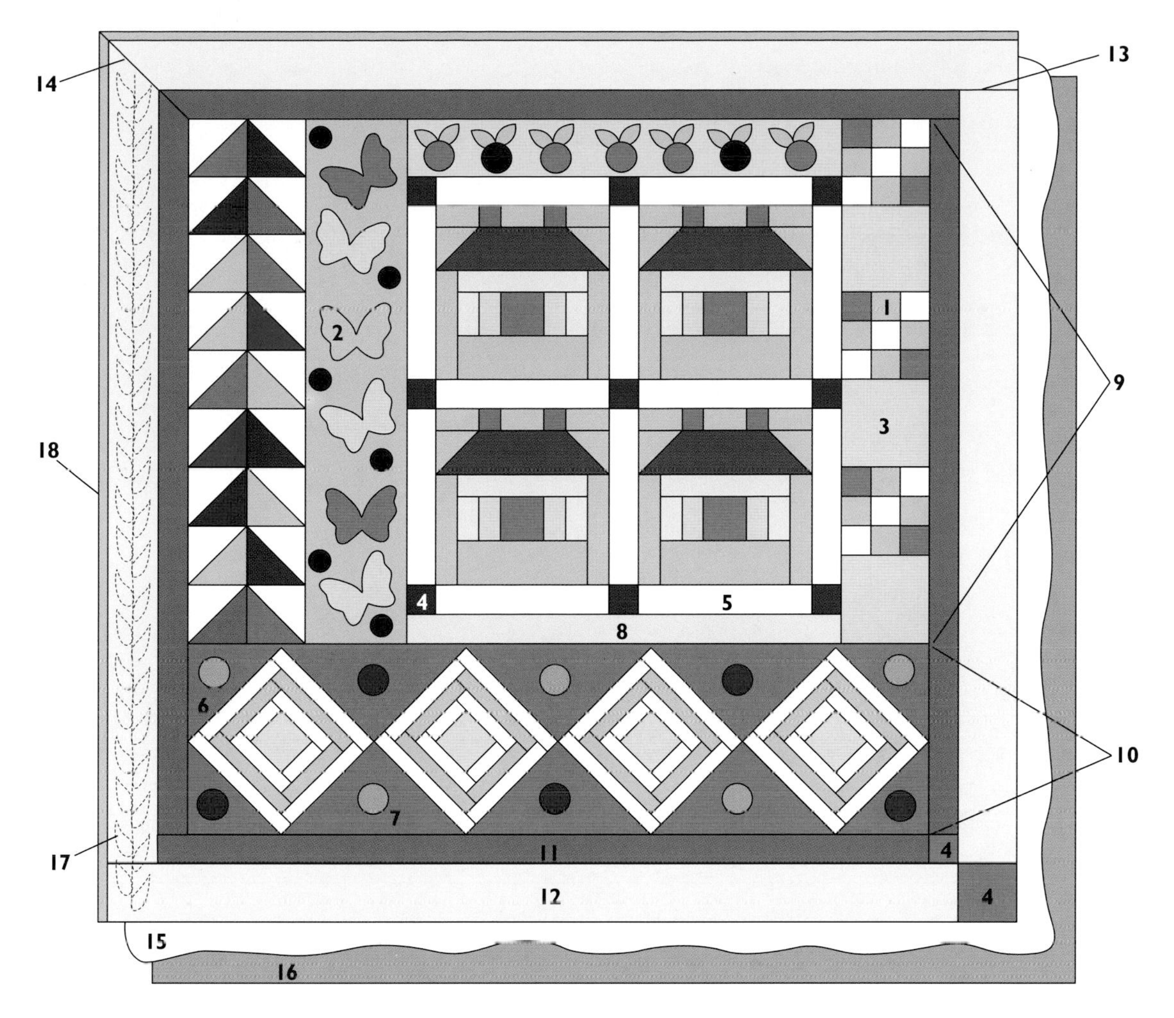

PARTS OF A QUILT

1. *Pieced block*
2. *Appliquéd motif*
3. *Alternate or plain block*
4. *Corner posts*
5. *Sashing or lattice*
6. *Corner triangles*
7. *Side triangles*
8. *Spacer*
9. *Straight set*
10. *Diagonal set*
11. *Inner border*
12. *Outer border*
13. *Straight border*
14. *Mitered border*
15. *Batting*
16. *Backing*
17. *Quilting design*
18. *Binding*

Planning

Planning your quilt can begin with a simple idea or theme, such as, "I want to make a quilt for my sister, and I know she likes blue and yellow." Or, perhaps, "I'll make a quilt to remind me of my favorite childhood vacations at the beach." Whatever that starting point is for you, let it lead you into designing a quilt that will complete your idea.

Some quiltmakers like to preplan and have a sense of what the finished quilt will look like. Graph paper can be helpful for making a sketch of the blocks and then playing with the many possible arrangements. This allows you not only to preview the end result, but also to see if there are any additional pieces needed (sashings, alternate blocks, and so on) to make all the pieces fit properly.

Another, more spontaneous approach is to make the blocks, and then let the design evolve, which is how we work. Often there are leftover blocks for other projects or perhaps a few more blocks are needed. In working this way, we let the blocks lead us in many interesting directions that we may not have considered if we had preplanned. We encourage you to try both ways, and then decide which works best for you.

Supplies and Equipment

You will need the following supplies and equipment to make the quilts featured in this book. There are a variety of brands but remember that good quality tools will make the project run more smoothly.

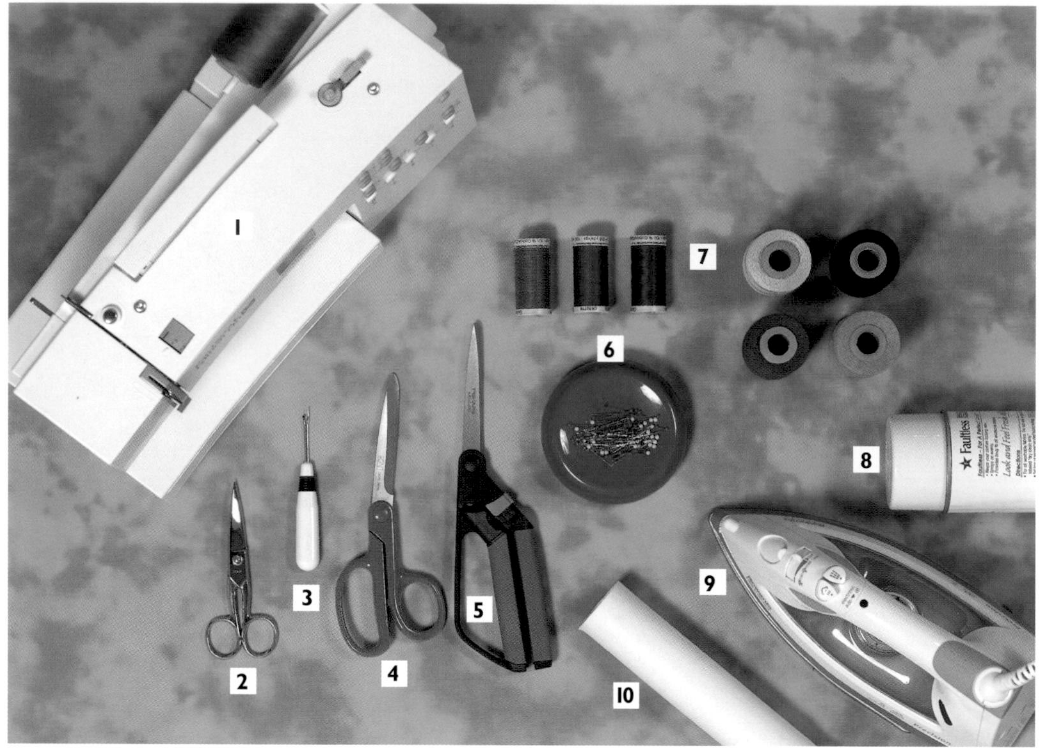

1. *Sewing machine*
2. *Small thread cutting scissors*
3. *Seam ripper*
4. *Paper scissors*
5. *Large fabric scissors*
6. *Fine glass-head pins*
7. *100% cotton thread*
8. *Spray starch or sizing*
9. *Steam iron*
10. *Fusible web or freezer-paper*

Shopping List

TO GET STARTED:

- ❏ Cutting mat
- ❏ Rotary cutter
- ❏ 6" x 6" square ruler
- ❏ 6" x 12" ruler
- ❏ fine glass-head pins
- ❏ 100% cotton thread
- ❏ Sewing machine or hand sewing needles
- ❏ Seam ripper
- ❏ Steam iron
- ❏ Spray starch or sizing
- ❏ Small thread cutting scissors

FOR APPLIQUÉ:

- ❏ Large fabric scissors
- ❏ Paper scissors
- ❏ Fusible web or plastic-coated freezer paper
- ❏ Template plastic
- ❏ Fine-line permanent pen

FOR FINISHING AND QUILTING:

- ❏ Reducing glass
- ❏ Tape measure
- ❏ Masking tape
- ❏ Batting

FOR HAND QUILTING:

- ❏ Cotton darning needles
- ❏ Chalk line markers
- ❏ Marking pencils
- ❏ Fabric markers
- ❏ Fabric eraser
- ❏ Quilting design template
- ❏ Quilting needles, Betweens
- ❏ Needle grabber or finger cots
- ❏ Thimble
- ❏ Quilting thread
- ❏ Quilting hoop

FOR MACHINE QUILTING:

- ❏ Safety pins
- ❏ Walking foot
- ❏ Darning foot

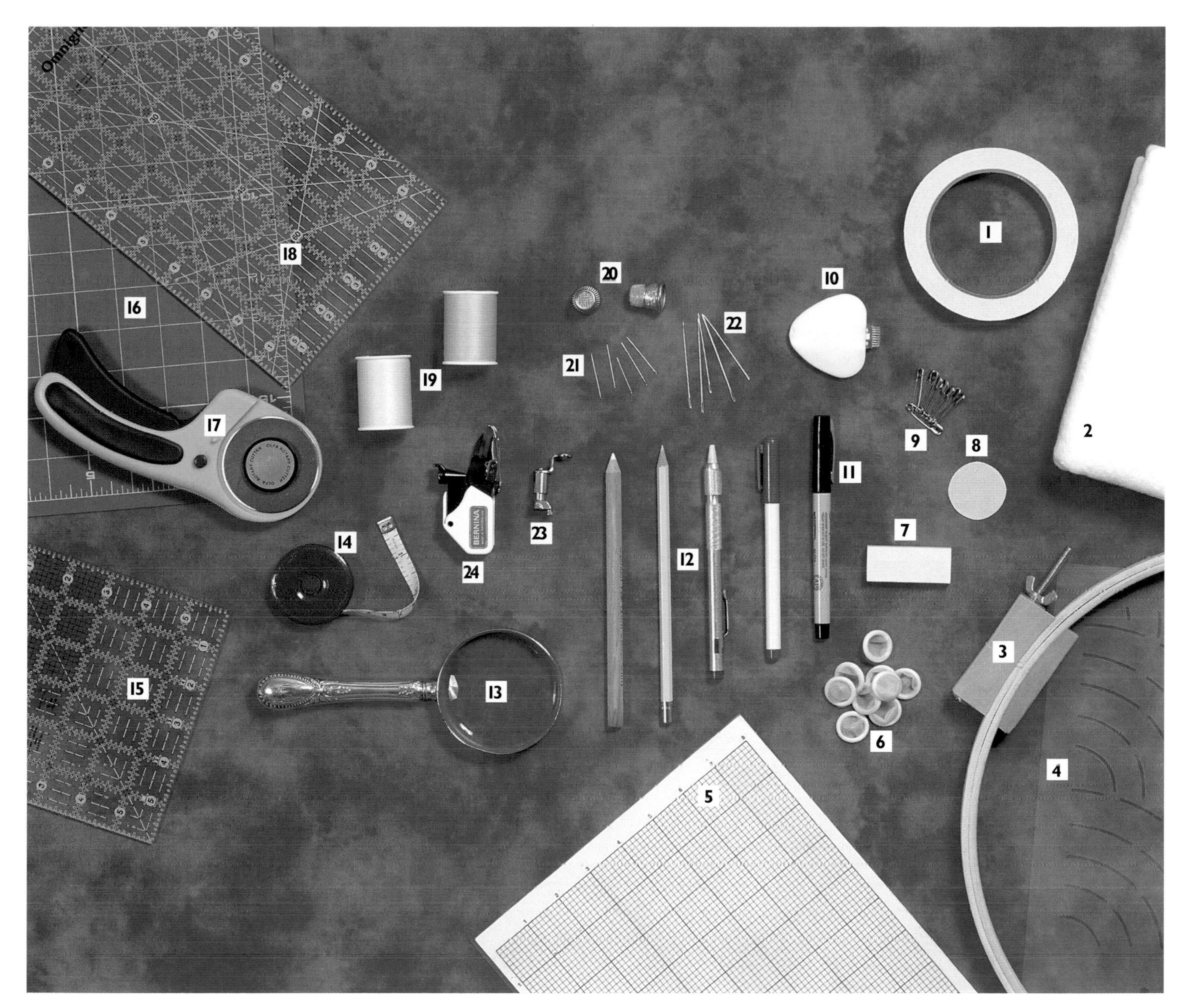

1. *Masking tape*
2. *Batting*
3. *Quilting hoop*
4. *Quilting template*
5. *Template plastic*
6. *Grabbers, finger cots*
7. *Fabric eraser*
8. *Needle grabber*
9. *Safety pins*
10. *Chalk line marker*
11. *Fine-line permanent pen*
12. *Fabric markers*
13. *Reducing glass*
14. *Tape measure*
15. *6" x 6" square ruler*
16. *Cutting mat*
17. *Rotary cutter*
18. *6" x 12" ruler*
19. *Quilting thread*
20. *Thimbles*
21. *Quilting needles*
22. *Cotton darning needles*
23. *Darning foot*
24. *Walking foot*

Studio Gardens, 48" x 45". Made by Anne Oldford; machine quilted by Kathy Sandbach.

Fabric Selection

Choosing the right combination of fabrics, in terms of both color and design, can be very challenging. The abundance of fabrics available, combined with our enjoyment of the full spectrum of color, creates an overwhelming number of possibilities when faced with selecting just the right combination of fabrics. We suggest you approach your project with a sense of your own style, color preference, and theme. Also, feel free to copy fabric and color combinations as you see them in this book or from other sources.

Many of the quilts in this book were inspired by a fabric or a combination of fabrics, while others were based on a theme that told a story to the viewer. Some quilts reflect a favorite season or place. One of our quilts was inspired by a garden and each fabric represents one of the flowerbeds. Whatever you want to say can be accomplished in fabric using the blocks we give you.

We suggest starting with three fabrics of varying values (one light, one medium, and one dark). If one of the fabrics best defines your theme, you can then select color families based on that particular piece. However, make sure you have several lights, mediums, and darks of each color.

The three stacks—light, medium, and dark—should be arranged from the very lightest and brightest to the dullest, darkest hue within each color family.

These three categories of color and value will insure your project has the proper light source and contrast, which are both important ingredients for a successful and exciting quilt. The mediums will provide the path between the light and dark in each block, creating the desired movement that provides interest to the viewer. Also, the light, medium, and dark combinations will provide an abundance of vitality, allow you to create a personal statement, and reflect your theme to its fullest. Enjoy choosing your fabric—this process can be the best part of quiltmaking!

The Patterns

The quilt block patterns were selected for this book because of their simplicity in both design and construction. The patterns are easy enough for the beginner, but even the experienced quiltmaker will enjoy working with the patterns as they allow for endless possibilities in fabric and color selection, as well as design options. Each pattern covers one of the basic techniques of block construction that we feel is important in building a solid foundation in quiltmaking.

The Nine-Patch Block and the Fence

CHAPTER 2

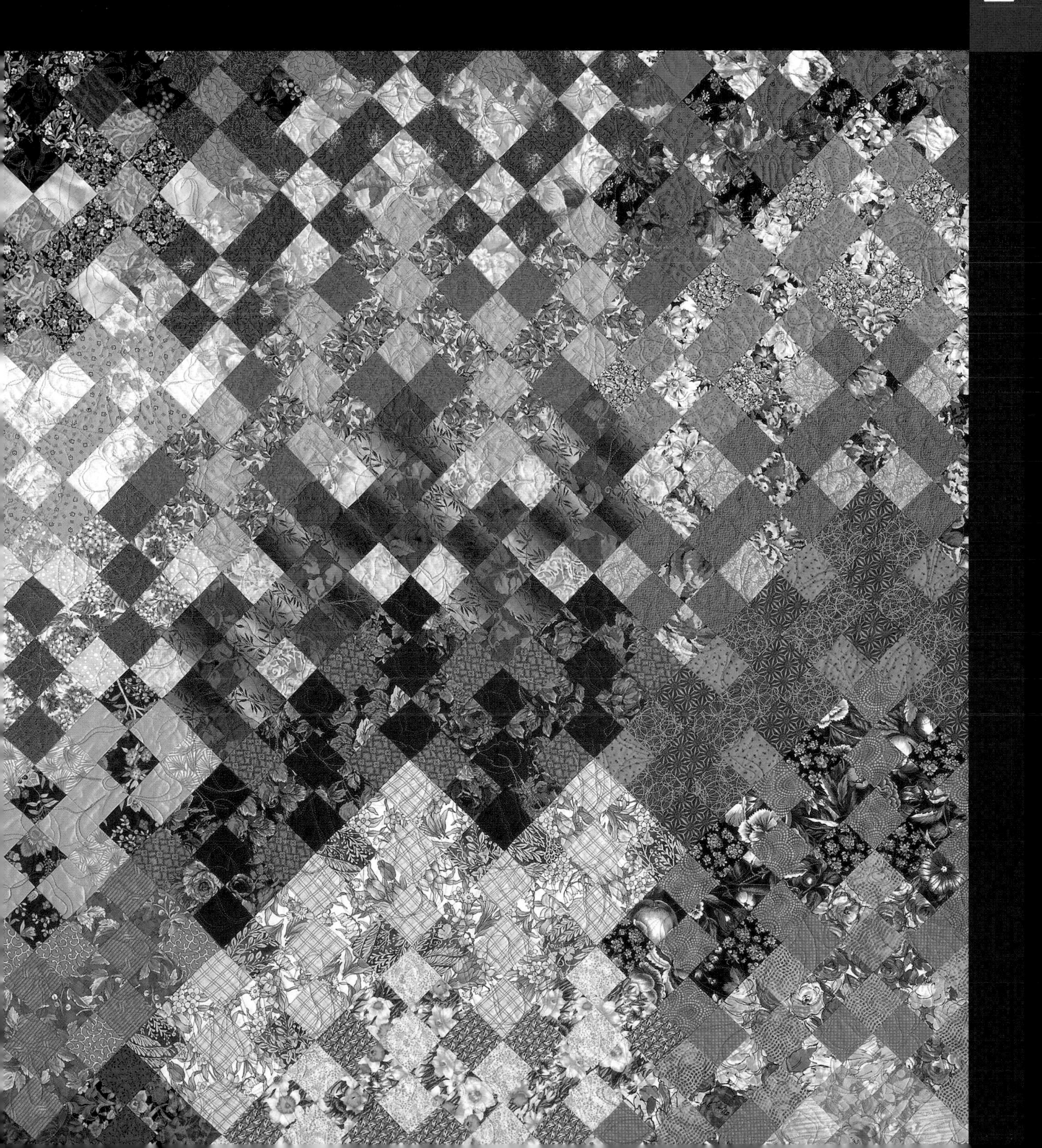

Nine-Patch Block

6" block

This simple variation on the traditional Nine-Patch block has a strong diagonal formed by color placement.

BLOCK SIZE: 6" finished
SHAPE: Square
TECHNIQUES: Quick-cutting and strip piecing
FABRIC SUGGESTIONS: Choose three fabrics: light, medium, and dark.

How to make a Nine-Patch

YARDAGE

To make eight blocks:
1/8 yard Fabric A
1/4 yard **each** Fabric B and C

A	B	C
B	C	B
C	B	A

CUTTING

(A) Cut one 2 1/2" strip.
(B) Cut two 2 1/2" strips (cut one strip in half to form two strips approximately 22" long).
(C) Cut two 2 1/2" strips (cut one strip in half to form two strips approximately 22" long).

CONSTRUCTION

1. Sew the strips together to make two set combinations, use half strips for Set Two.

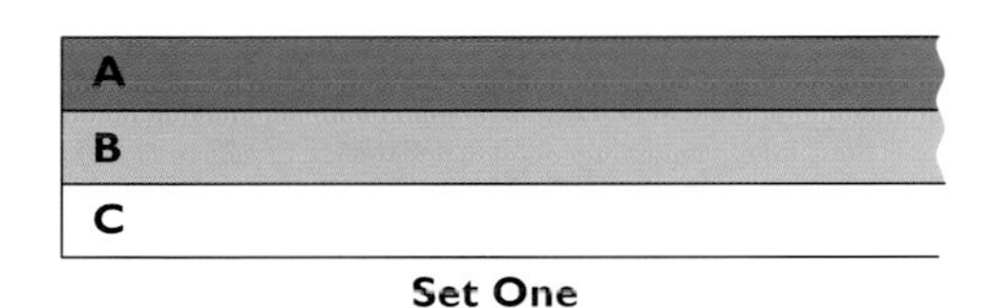

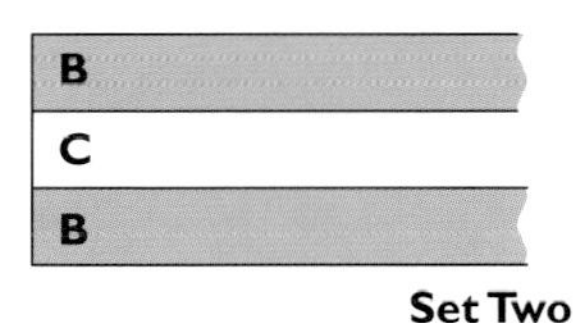

2. Press the seams in the directions indicated by the arrows. If Fabric C is the darkest fabric, then reverse the pressing direction (see page 98 for help if needed).

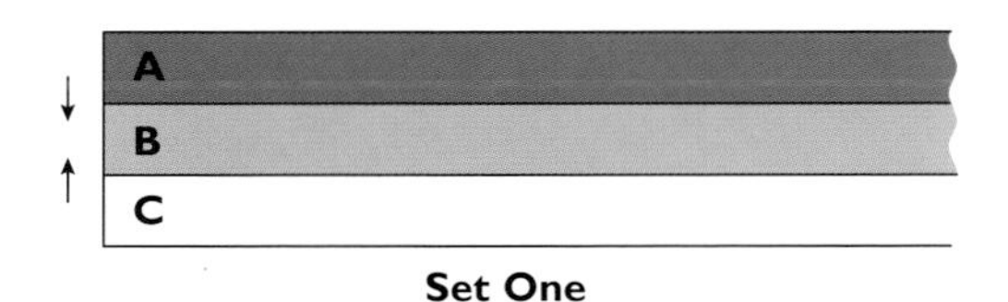

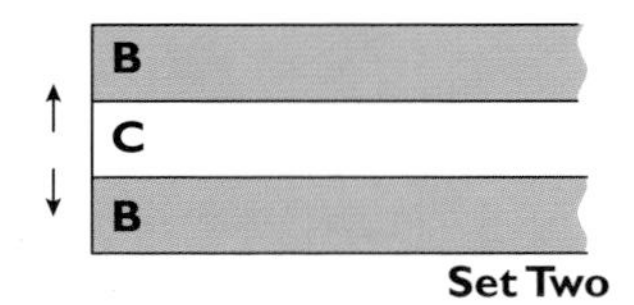

3. Remove the selvages and cut the sets apart every 2 1/2", to make units.

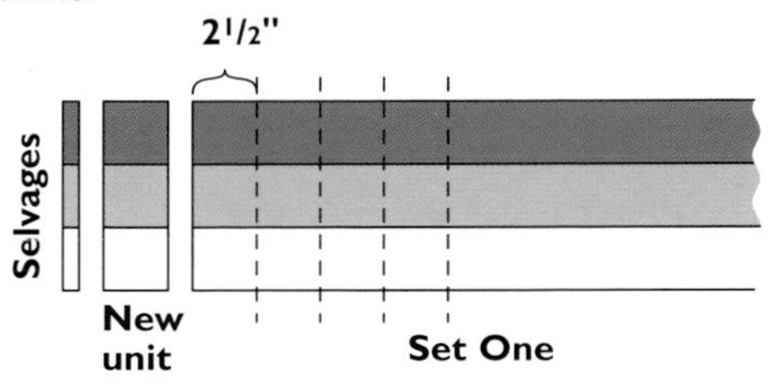

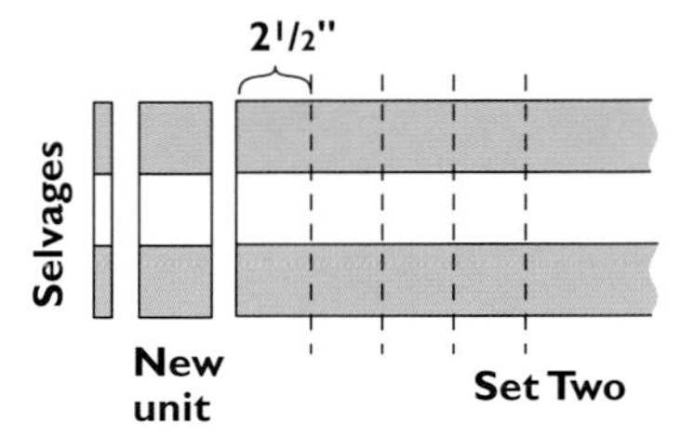

4. Join the units to make completed blocks.

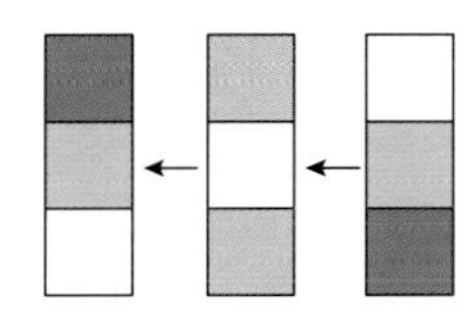

HELPFUL HINT

Place pins at the intersections and at opposite ends. This will keep the edges of the block straight and prevent the seam allowances from slipping.

5. Press the seams first on the wrong side, then on the right side in the direction indicated by the arrows (see page 98 for help if needed).

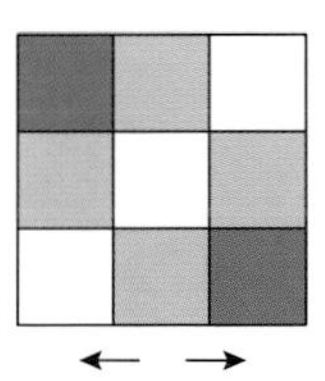

CHECKPOINT: The blocks should measure 6 1/2". Straighten the edges with the cutting tools if necessary.

HELPFUL HINT

Cutting instructions for making more blocks are found in the cutting chart on page 21.

The Fence

3 1/2"-wide Fence

The fence is a versatile addition to a pieced quilt. It can be used as an extension of one of the blocks or as sashing or a border.

SIZE: 3 1/2" wide x finished length. (The railing width and length vary with each individual project.)

SHAPES: Rectangles

TECHNIQUES: Quick-cutting and strip piecing

FABRIC SUGGESTIONS: Choose two or more contrasting fabrics.

How to make the Fence

YARDAGE

To make a 72" length of fence:

$^1/_4$ yard **each** of one light fabric and one dark fabric

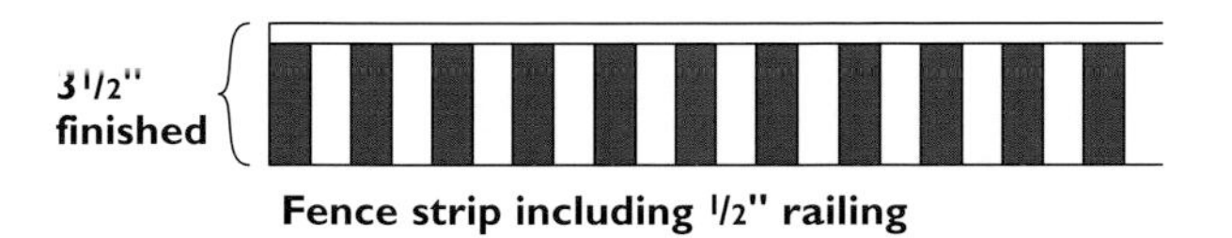

CUTTING

Light fabric: Cut three $1^1/_2$" strips.

Dark fabric: Cut three $1^1/_2$" strips.

Light or dark (for railing): Cut two 1" strips.

CONSTRUCTION

HELPFUL HINT

Cut the strips in half to make 22" (approximate) lengths to prevent the strips from stretching when sewn into sets.

1. Sew alternating strips of three light and three dark strips together to make a set of six strips, as shown.

2. Carefully press the seams in the direction of the darker strips.

CHECKPOINT: The width of the set should measure $6^1/_2$".

3. Remove the selvages and cut the sets apart every $3^1/_2$".

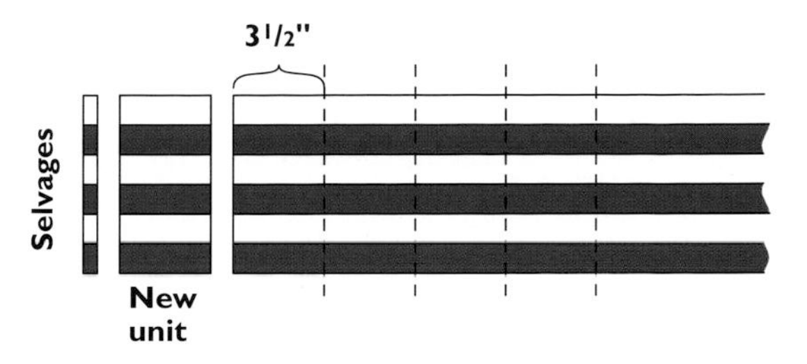

4. Determine the length of the fence. Remove the selvages from the railing strips and sew them together end to end. Cut them the predetermined length.

5. Join the fence units together to fit the length of the railing.

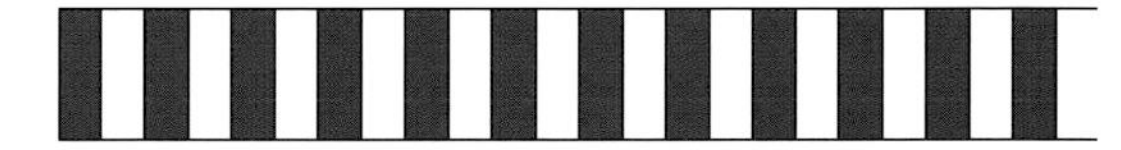

HELPFUL HINT

To prevent stretching, piece the railing strip to the needed length. Pin and then sew it to the fence. If the fence is too long for the railing, it is better to make a few seams where the strips are joined a bit wider rather than trying to ease in extra fullness, which will cause rippling.

6. Sew the railing to the fence units. Press the seam toward the railing.

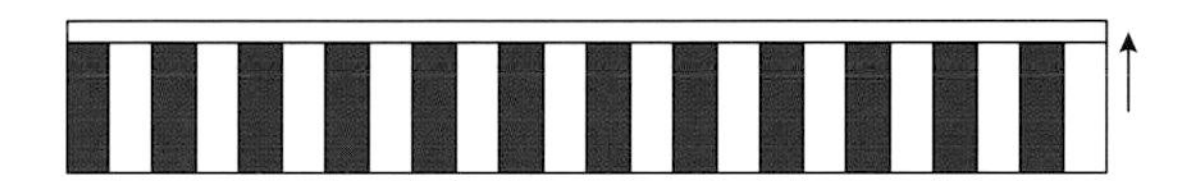

CHECKPOINT: The width of the fence should measure 4" wide and is ready to be used in your project.

Chicken Yard

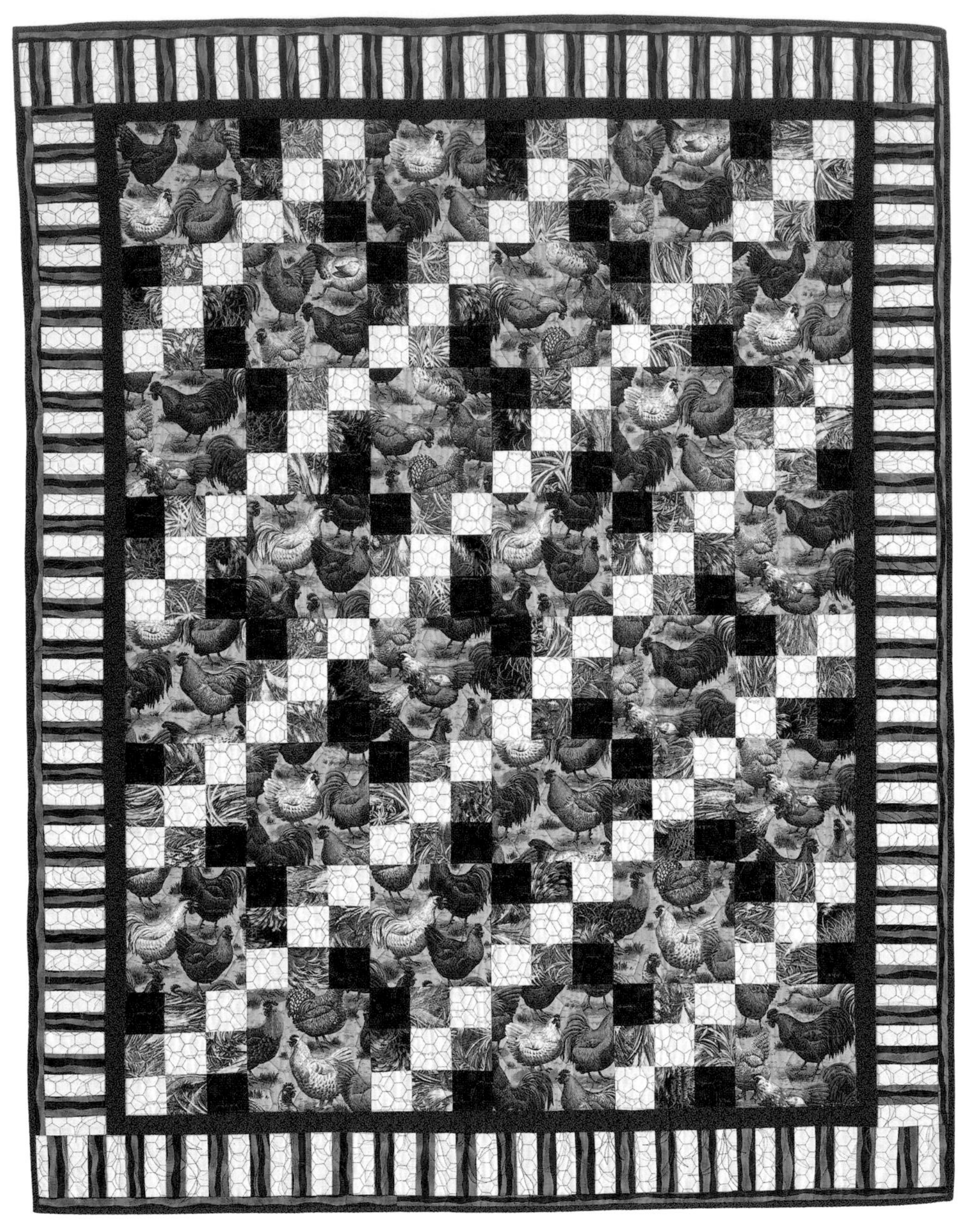

Chicken Yard, 45" x 57". Made by Diana McClun and Laura Nownes; machine quilted by Kathy Sandbach.

PATTERN: Nine-Patch

A	B	C
B	C	B
C	B	A

BLOCK SIZE: 6" finished

SETTING: Straight with alternate blocks

TECHNIQUES: Quick-cutting and strip piecing

FABRIC AND COLOR INSPIRATION: The rooster and chicken printed fabric established the theme for choosing the fabrics used in the Nine-Patch blocks.

	Photo quilt	Twin	Queen
Finished size	45" x 57"	69" x 87"	87" x 87"
Blocks set	6 x 8	10 x 13	13 x13
Number of Nine-Patch blocks	24	65	84
Number of alternate blocks	24	65	85

YARDAGE

Based on 42" wide fabric, from selvage to selvage

	Photo quilt	Twin	Queen
NINE-PATCHES:			
Dark fabric (A)	3/8	3/4	1 1/8
Medium fabric (B)	5/8	1 1/2	1 3/4
Light fabric (C)	1/2	1 1/8	1 1/4
Alternate blocks:	1 1/8	2 1/4	3
Inner border:			
Cut crosswise and pieced	1/4	1/2	1/2
or Cut lengthwise	1 3/8	2 1/4	2 1/4
FENCE:			
Light fabric	1/2	3/4	3/4
Dark fabric (including railing)	7/8	1 1/4	1 1/4
Backing	3	5 1/4	7 3/4
Binding (1/4" finished)	3/8	1/2	5/8

CUTTING

Use Quick-cutting techniques on page 95.

	Photo quilt	Twin	Queen
NINE-PATCHES:			
Dark fabric (A)			
Number of 2 1/2" strips	3	9	11
Medium fabric (B)			
Number of 2 1/2" strips	6	18	22
Light fabric (C)			
Number of 2 1/2" strips	5	14	17
***Alternate blocks:**			
Number of 6 1/2" strips	4	11	15
Cut strips into 6 1/2" squares	24	65	85
Inner border: Number of 1 1/2" strips			
Cut crosswise	5	8	8
or Cut lengthwise	4	4	4
FENCE:			
Light fabric: Number of 1 1/2" strips	9	15	15
Dark fabric: Number of 1 1/2" strips	9	15	15
Dark Railing: Number of 1" strips	5	8	9
Backing: Piecing Diagram page 103	B	A	C

HELPFUL HINT

*Alternate blocks should be cut after Nine-Patches are constructed in case any size adjustment is necessary. See the Checkpoint in the next column.

CONSTRUCTION

Refer to the instructions on page 15 for help, if needed.

1. Make the required number of Nine-Patch blocks, as indicated. Sew the 2 1/2" strips of light, medium and dark fabrics into combinations as shown. Refer to the chart below to determine the number of sets required for your desired quilt size.

Set One	Set Two
A	B
B	C
C	B

	Photo quilt	Twin	Queen
Set One	3	9	11
Set Two	1 1/2	4 1/2	5 1/2

CHECKPOINT

The Nine-Patch blocks should measure 6 1/2". If they are all a bit small, cut the alternate blocks to the size of your blocks.

2. Lay out all of the Nine-Patch and alternate blocks in a straight set, referring to the photo for placement. Sew the blocks together in rows. Sew the rows together. Refer to the instructions on page 101 for help, if needed.

3. Attach the side inner borders, using an average measurement of the sides to determine the length. Then attach the top and bottom inner borders. Refer to the instructions on page 102 for help, if needed.

4. Construct the fence borders. Sew them to the sides and then the top and bottom of the quilt, as shown.

FINISHING

Refer to the Backing Fabric and Batting, page 103. Quilt as preferred, see instructions on page 104, if needed. Refer to the Binding instructions, page 106.

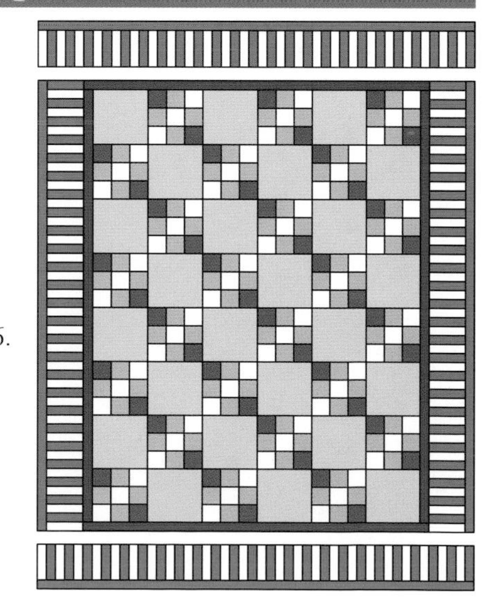

Flight of the Red Birds

Flight of the Red Birds, 84" x 84". Made by Diana McClun and Laura Nownes; machine quilted by Kathy Sandbach.

PATTERNS: Nine-Patch and Appliquéd bird

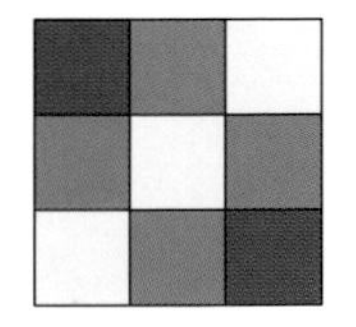

BLOCK SIZES: 6" finished

SETTING: Straight

TECHNIQUES: Quick-cutting, strip piecing, and appliqué

FABRIC AND COLOR INSPIRATION: Choose many different fabrics that represent branches, trees, and pinecones, in both warm and cool colors, and in light and dark values. The contrast between light and dark creates the interesting design of this quilt. The white background for the birds adds sparkle as well as a path for the flight of the birds.

	Crib/Wall	Twin	Photo quilt
Finished size	48" x 60"	72" x 84"	84" x 84"
Blocks set	8 x 10	12 x 14	14 x 14
Number of Nine-Patch blocks	60	132	156
Number of Bird blocks	20	36	40

An abundance of fabrics will achieve the look of this quilt. Generous amounts of yardage are suggested. Leftover pieces can be added to your scrap basket for another project.

Several combinations of fabrics are used to create the Nine-Patch blocks. Refer to the diagram on page 22 for the placement of the blocks.

YARDAGE

Based on 42" wide fabric, from selvage to selvage

NINE-PATCHES:			
*Combinations 1 and 8: 3 fabrics **each**	1/4	3/8	5/8
Combination 2: 3 fabrics **each**	1/4	1/4	1/4
Combination 3: 3 fabrics **each**	3/8	3/8	3/8
*Combinations 4 and 10: 3 fabrics **each**	3/8	5/8	3/4
*Combinations 5, 7 and 11: 3 fabrics **each**	3/8	7/8	1
Combination 6: 3 fabrics **each**	1/4	5/8	3/4
Combination 9: 3 fabrics **each**	----	1/4	3/8
BIRD BLOCKS:			
Background	1	1 3/8	1 1/2
Birds	5/8	7/8	1
Backing	3	5	7 1/2
Binding (1/4" finished)	1/2	5/8	5/8

*Same fabrics used for these combinations.

Note: There are no combinations 8, 10, or 11 used in the crib/wall size.

CUTTING

Use Quick-cutting techniques on page 95.

NINE-PATCHES:			
Number of blocks:			
Combinations 1 **and** 8	4	16	20
Combination 2	8	8	8
Combination 3	12	12	12
Combinations 4 **and** 10	16	24	28
Combinations 5, 7, **and** 11	12	40	48
Combination 6	8	24	28
Combination 9	---	8	12
Number of 2 1/2" strips for combinations with:	**Fabric A**	**Fabric B**	**Fabric C**
Four blocks	1	2	2
Eight blocks	1	2	2
Twelve blocks	2	4	3
Sixteen blocks	2	4	3
Twenty blocks	3	6	5
Twenty-four blocks	3	6	5
Twenty-eight blocks	4	8	6
Forty blocks	5	10	8
Forty-eight blocks	6	12	9
BIRD BLOCKS:			
White Background:			
Number of 6 1/2" strips	4	6	7
Cut strips into 6 1/2" squares	20	36	40
Bird Pattern page 108	10 & 10R*	18 & 18R*	20 & 20R*
Backing: Piecing Diagram page 103	B	B	C

*R= reverse template on fabric.

CONSTRUCTION

1. Make the Nine-Patch blocks. See the instructions on page 15 for help, if needed.

2. Make the appliquéd bird blocks using your preferred method of appliqué, referring to page 98 for help if needed. A machine-blanket stitch was used around the edge of the birds.

3. Refer to the Block Combination Layout diagram and the photo of the quilt for the placement of the blocks. Sew the pieced and appliquéd blocks together to complete the quilt top. Refer to page 101 for help, if needed.

FINISHING

Refer to the Backing Fabric and Batting, page 103. Quilt as preferred, see instructions on page 104 if needed. Refer to the Binding instructions on page 106.

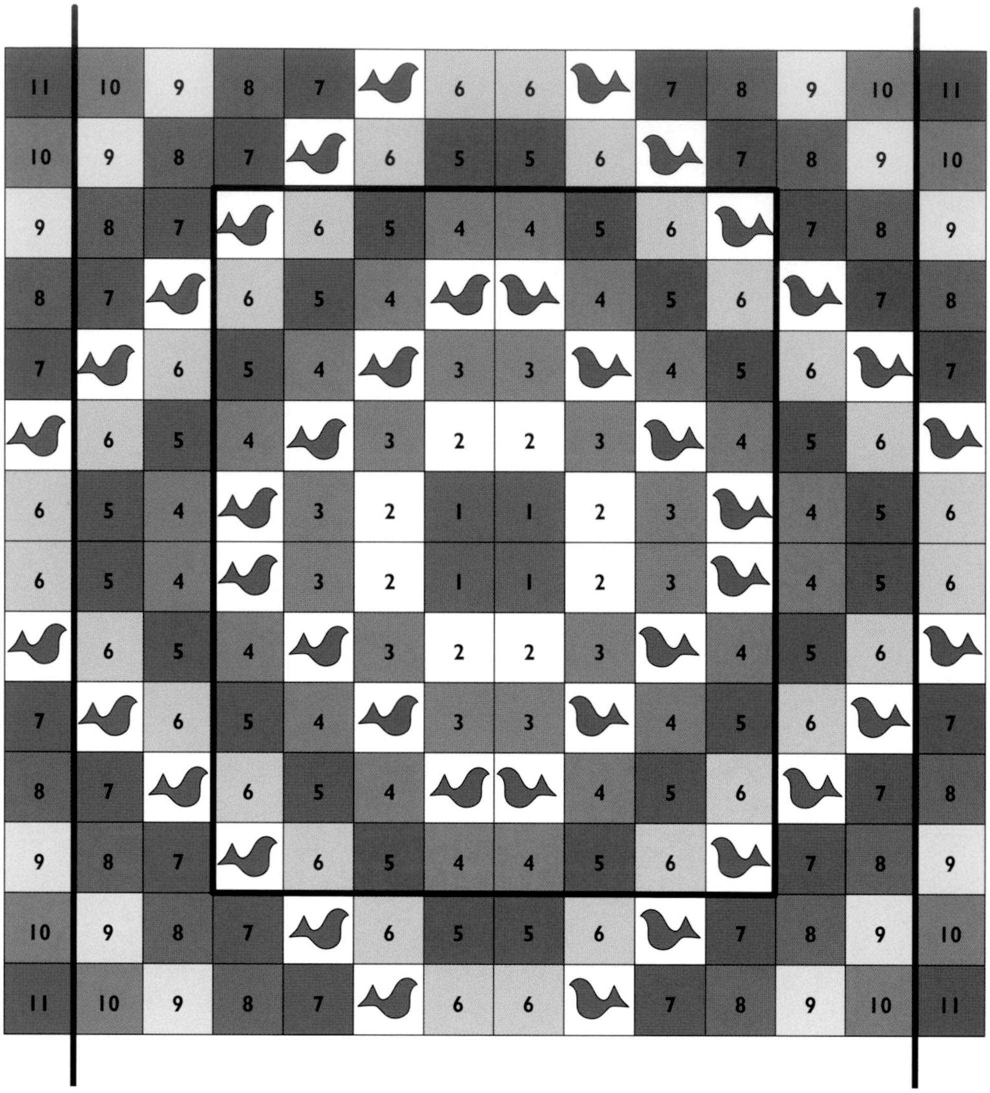

Block combination layout diagram for crib, twin, and photo sizes

Nine-Patch Flower Bed

The Nine-Patch Flower Bed, 68" x 76½". Made by Diana McClun and Laura Nownes; machine quilted by Kathy Sandbach.

PATTERN: Nine-Patch

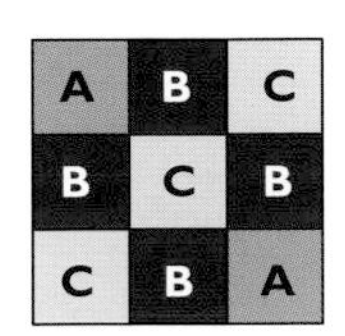

BLOCK SIZE: 6" finished

SETTING: Diagonal

TECHNIQUES: Quick-cutting, strip piecing, and quarter-square triangles

FABRIC AND COLOR INSPIRATION: All of the fabrics were chosen from a collection of realistic floral prints in both small and large scale, warm and cool colors, light and dark values. The fabric combinations in the blocks were organized to simulate beds of flowers.

	Photo quilt	Queen
Finished size	68" x 76$^{1}/_{2}$"	85" x 85"
Blocks set	8 x 9	10 x 10
Number of blocks	128	181
Number of side setting triangles	30	36

Helpful Hint

To achieve the same look as in the photo, a variety of fabrics is required. There will be extra blocks. Organize your fabrics into combinations of three, referring to the chart below to determine the total number of combinations required for your desired quilt size. Use scraps from your stash, or if you choose to purchase fabric, requirements for **each** combination are listed below.

YARDAGE

Based on 42" fabric, from selvage to selvage

NINE-PATCH BLOCKS:

Number of combinations:	25	38
For **each** combination:		
Fabric A	$^{1}/_{8}$	$^{1}/_{8}$
Fabric B	$^{1}/_{4}$	$^{1}/_{4}$
Fabric C	$^{1}/_{4}$	$^{1}/_{4}$
Setting triangles:	1	1$^{1}/_{4}$
Backing	4	7$^{1}/_{2}$
Binding ($^{1}/_{4}$" finished)	$^{1}/_{2}$	$^{5}/_{8}$

CUTTING

Use Quick-cutting techniques found on page 95.

NINE-PATCH BLOCKS:

For **each** combination		
Number of 2$^{1}/_{2}$" strips:		
Fabric A	1	1
Fabric B	2	2
Fabric C	2	2
Side setting triangles:		
Number of 10$^{1}/_{2}$" strips	2	3
Cut into 10$^{1}/_{2}$" squares	8	9
Cut the squares into quarters diagonally.		
Corner triangles:		
Number of 6" squares	2	2
Cut the squares in half diagonally.		
Backing: Piecing Diagram page 103	B	C

CONSTRUCTION

1. Make the Nine-Patch blocks referring to the instructions on page 15 for help, if needed.

2. A design wall is very helpful when arranging the blocks. Refer to the diagram below and photo for placement of the blocks from **each** combination. Note that the additional Nine-Patch blocks are used along the edges.

Queen size

3. Sew the blocks together with the side and corner triangles in a diagonal setting, referring to the instructions on page 102, if needed.

Helpful Hint

Due to the number of seams in this quilt, it is impossible to preplan the pressing direction to insure alternating seam allowances at each of the intersections. Pin at each intersection, since many of the intersections have seam allowances pressed in the same direction. When joining the blocks into rows, do not press the new seams until after the entire quilt top is sewn together. This gives you the ability to turn the seams while sewing.

Note

The side setting triangles were cut larger than needed to allow for straightening the edges. Use the cutting tools to trim the excess fabric $^{1}/_{2}$" beyond the outer corners of the blocks. See diagram at bottom of page 55 for help if needed.

FINISHING

Refer to the Backing Fabric and Batting instructions on page 103. Quilt as preferred, see the instructions page 104, if needed. Refer to the Binding instructions on page 106.

CHAPTER 3

Half-Square Triangles

Half-Square Triangle

4" block

The half-square triangle is a simple block that offers many setting options, from traditional to abstract.

BLOCK SIZE: 4" finished
SHAPE: Triangle
TECHNIQUES: Quick-cutting and half-square triangles
FABRIC SUGGESTIONS: Choose one dark fabric and one light fabric for each block.

How to make Half-Square Triangles

YARDAGE

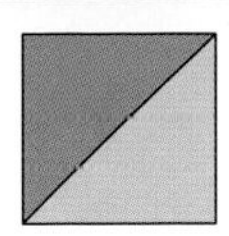

To make sixteen blocks:
1/4 yard **each** of two fabrics, one light and one dark

CUTTING

Light and dark fabric:
Cut one 5" strip of **each** fabric.
Cut the strips into 5" squares.
Cut the squares in half diagonally.

Helpful Hint

To cut light and dark fabric together: Cut the fabrics in half to make two pieces approximately 9" x 22". Place and press the fabric pieces right sides facing each other and aligning the selvage edges. Cut a 5" strip. Cut the strip into 5" squares, and then cut the squares in half diagonally. The cut triangles are conveniently layered (light and dark) and ready for sewing.

Note

We find this method for making half-square triangles more accurate than other methods we have tried.

CONSTRUCTION

1. Place a light fabric and a dark fabric triangle right sides together.
2. Stitch the triangles together along the long side.

Helpful Hint

Several blocks can be sewn in a "chain," leaving a few stitches between blocks.

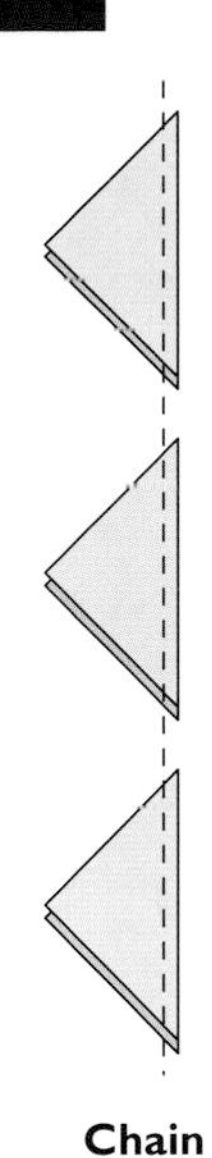

Chain

3. Cut the chained blocks apart.
4. With the darker triangle on top, place the unopened block onto the pressing board. Press the seam allowance flat on the wrong side to set the stitches. Then carefully lift the darker triangle and press it over the seam allowance, in the directions indicated by the arrows. Pressing in this manner will prevent distortion of the blocks.

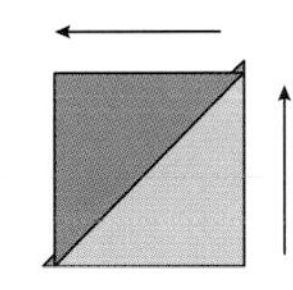

5. Place the block onto the cutting mat. Position the 6" x 6" square ruler over the block, with the 45° angle directly over the seam, as shown. Ideally, there should be excess fabric extending beyond the top and right-hand edges of the ruler, as well as the 4 1/2" markings on the left side and bottom edges.

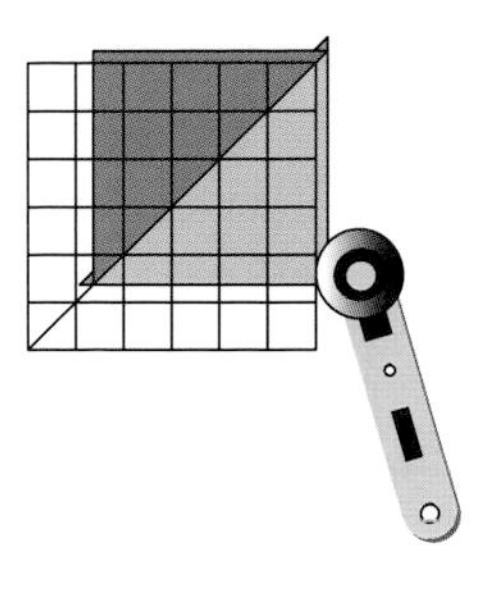

6. Use the rotary cutter to trim the excess fabric beyond the right and top edges as well as removing the corner extension of the seam allowance.

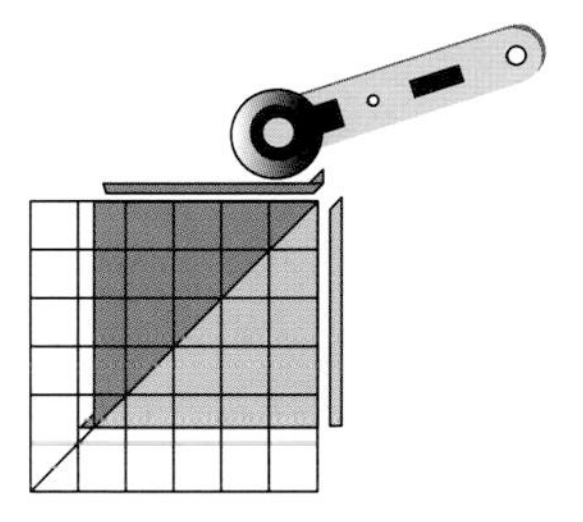

7. Rotate the block so that the clean-cut edges are positioned on the left and bottom. Reposition the ruler, again aligning the 45° angle with the diagonal seam. The straight edges on the left and bottom should be directly in line with the 4 1/2" markings on the ruler.

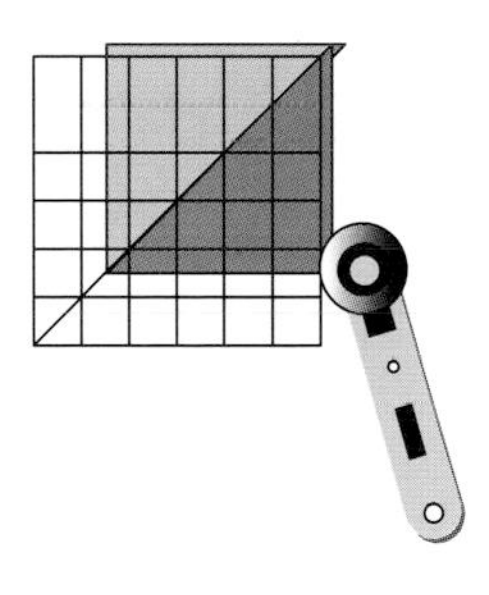

8. Use the rotary cutter to trim the excess fabric beyond the right and top edges of the block, as well as the corner extension of the seam allowance.

Checkpoint: The block should accurately measure 4 1/2" and is ready to be used in your project.

Scenes of Winter

Scenes of Winter, 64" x 64". Made by Diana McClun and Laura Nownes; machine quilted by Kathy Sandbach.

PATTERN: Half-Square triangle

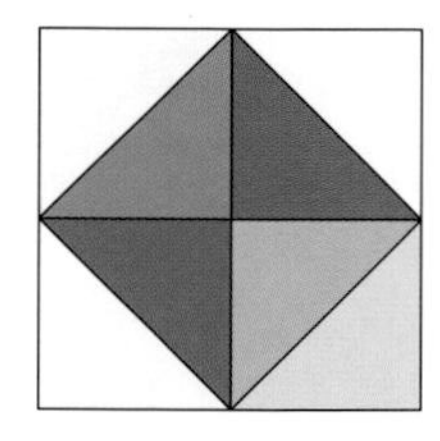

BLOCK SIZE: 8" finished

SETTING: Straight

TECHNIQUES: Quick-cutting and half-square triangles

FABRIC AND COLOR INSPIRATION:

We used a fabric collection of small winter scenes with snowflakes, evergreen trees, Canadian geese, and bare tree branches in colors that give warmth and dimension to the snow.

	Photo quilt	Queen	King
Finished size	64" x 64"	88" x 88"	104" x 104"
Blocks set	7 x 7	10 x 10	12 x 12
Number of blocks	49	100	144
Number of half-square triangles	196	400	576

YARDAGE

Based on 42" wide fabric, from selvage to selvage

HALF-SQUARE TRIANGLES:			
Light fabrics to total	2	$3^3/4$	$5^1/4$
Dark fabrics to total	2	$3^3/4$	$5^1/4$
Border:			
Cut crosswise	1	$1^1/4$	$1^5/8$
or Cut lengthwise	$1^7/8$	$2^1/2$	3
Backing	4	8	$9^1/8$
Binding ($^1/4$" finished)	$^1/2$	$^5/8$	$^3/4$

CUTTING

Use Quick-cutting techniques on page 95.

HALF-SQUARE TRIANGLES:			
Light and dark fabrics			
Number of 5" strips **each**:	13	25	36
Cut strips into 5" squares. Then cut squares in half diagonally.			
Border: number of $4^1/2$" strips			
Cut crosswise	6	9	11
or Cut lengthwise	4	4	4
Backing: Piecing Diagram page 103	A	C	C

CONSTRUCTION

1. Using the light and dark triangles, make the required number of Half-Square triangle blocks. Refer to the instructions on page 27 for help, if necessary.

2. Arrange and sew four blocks together as shown. Press the seams as indicated by the arrows.

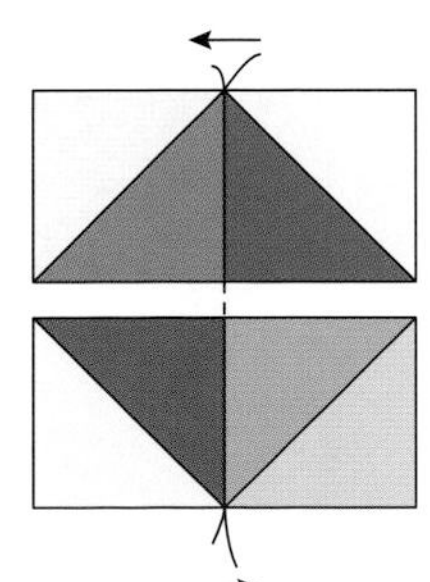

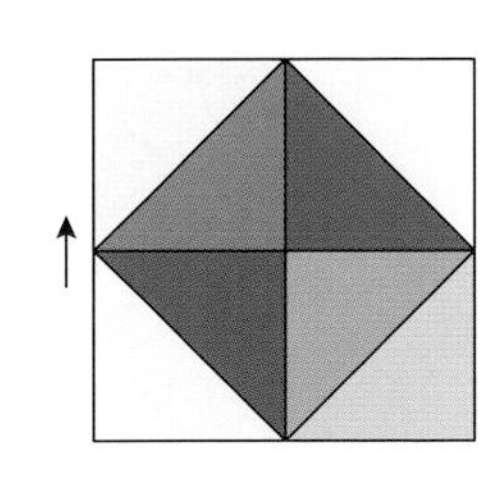

✔ CHECKPOINT: Each block should measure $8^1/2$" square.

3. Arrange the blocks, referring to the photo for placement. A design wall is especially helpful when determining the placement of the blocks.

4. Sew the blocks together in rows. Alternate the pressing direction of the seams to eliminate excess bulk at the intersections. Sew the rows together.

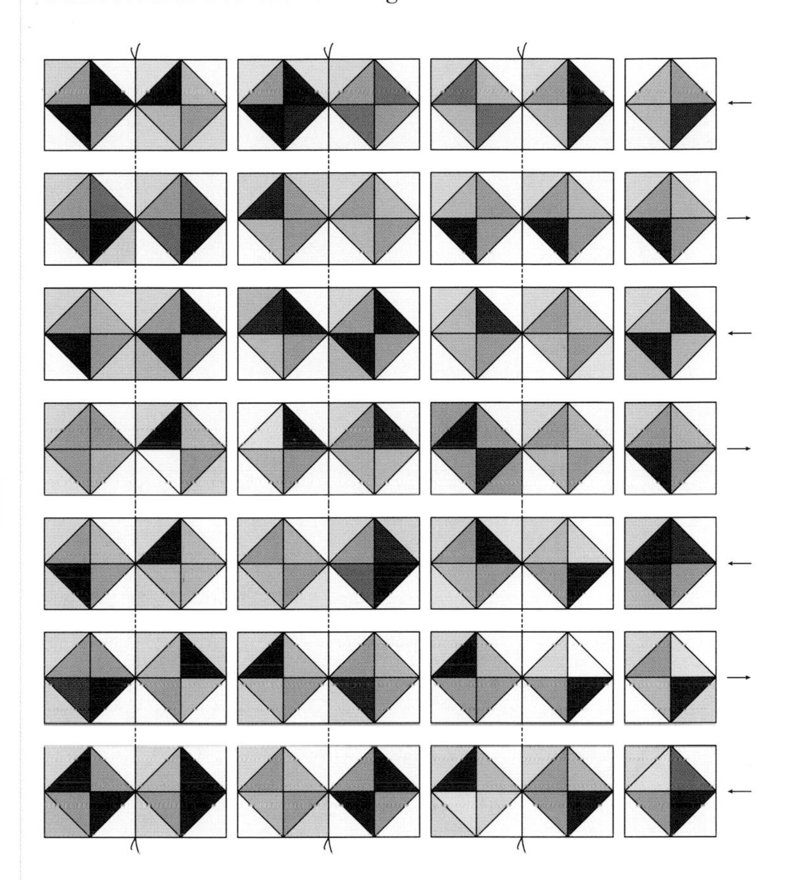

5. Attach the border strips, first to the sides and then to the top and bottom, to complete the quilt top. Refer to instructions on page 102 for help, if needed.

FINISHING

Refer to the Backing Fabric and Batting instructions on page 103. Quilt as preferred, see the instructions on page 104, if needed. Refer to the Binding instructions on page 106.

Historic Stars

Historic Stars, 66" x 86½". Made by Diana McClun and Laura Nownes; machine quilted by Kathy Sandbach.

PATTERN: Half-Square triangle

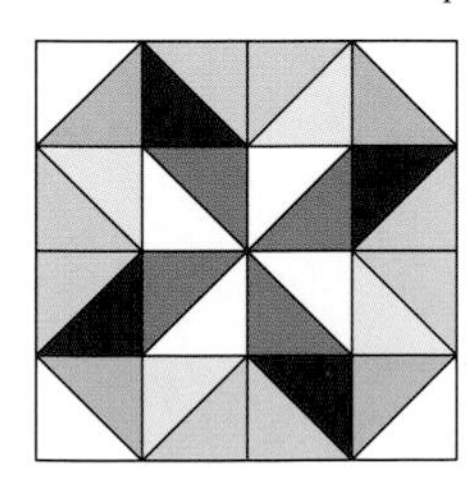

BLOCK SIZES: 16" finished

SETTING: Straight with sashing and corner posts

TECHNIQUES: Quick-cutting and half-square triangles

FABRIC AND COLOR INSPIRATION: A collection of reproduction fabrics in red, dark blue, beige, and brown were used to carry out the theme for these Civil War stars.

Three traditional block names for this pattern are: *Barbara Frietsche Star, Pieced Star* and *Yankee Puzzle.*

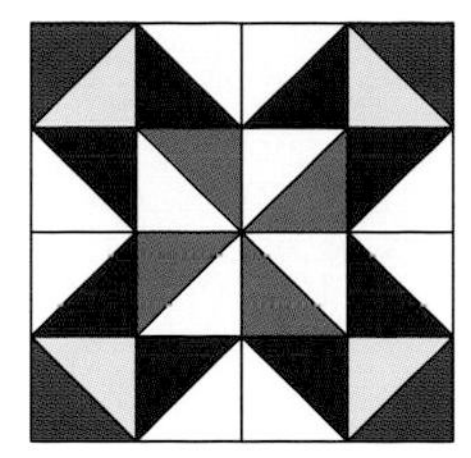
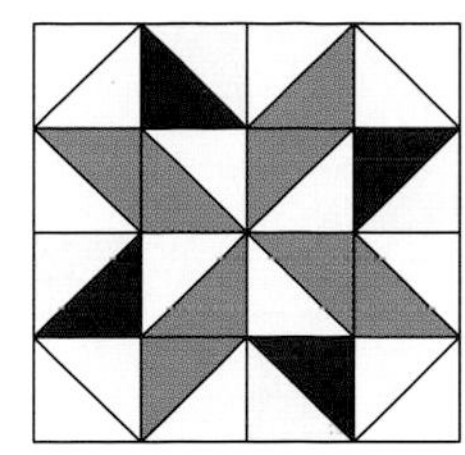
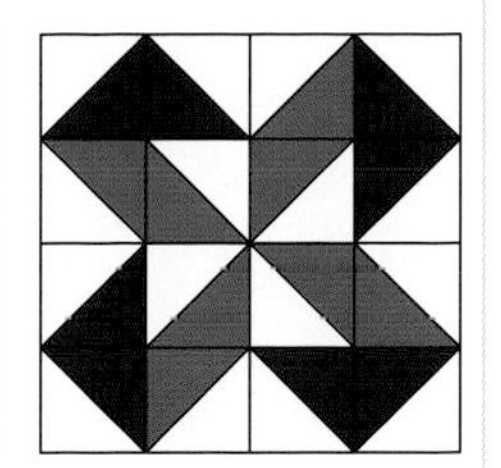

★**Barbara Frietsche Star** **Pieced Star** **Yankee Puzzle**

	Photo quilt	**Queen**	**King**
Finished size	66" x 86 1/2"	86 1/2" x 86 1/2"	107" x 107"
Blocks set	3 x 4	4 x 4	5 x 5
Number of blocks	12	16	25
Number of Half-Square triangles	192	256	400

YARDAGE

Based on 42" wide fabric, from selvage to selvage

HALF-SQUARE TRIANGLES:

Light, medium, and dark fabrics to total	4	5	8
Sashing	2	2 1/2	4
Posts	5/8	3/4	7/8
Backing	5 1/4	7 3/4	9 1/2
Binding (1/4" finished)	1/2	5/8	3/4

CUTTING

Use Quick-cutting techniques on page 95.

HALF-SQUARE TRIANGLES:

Number of 5" strips	24	32	50
Cut strips into 5" squares. Cut squares in half diagonally.			
Sashing: Number of 16 1/2" strips	4	5	8
Cut into 5" x 16 1/2" pieces	31	40	60
Posts: Number of 5" strips	3	4	5
Cut strips into 5" squares	20	25	36
Backing: Piecing Diagram page 103	B	C	C

CONSTRUCTION

1. Make the required number of Half-Square triangle blocks. Refer to the instructions on page 27 for help, if needed.

2. A design wall is very helpful to lay out all of the blocks. Refer to the diagrams to the left for suggested placement to make a variety of star patterns. The exact placement of the light and the dark triangles is important to the individual patterns.

Helpful Hint

Alternate the pressing direction of the seams at the intersections to eliminate bulk. It will be necessary to place a pin at each intersection to keep opposing seams close together and avoid slipping.

3. Sew the Half-Square triangles together to make the desired star blocks.

4. Sew the blocks together with sashing strips. Press the seams in the direction of the sashing strips.

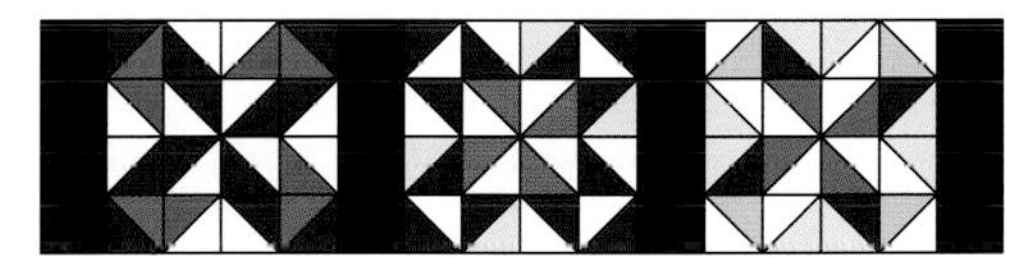

5. Construct the sashing and post units, as shown. Press the seams in the direction of the sashing strips.

6. Join the rows of blocks to the sashing/post strips to complete the quilt top.

★A Bit of History

Barbara Frietsche, born in 1766 is one of the most famous heroines in American literature. At the age of 95 she refused to lower her Union flag during the Confederate occupation of Frederick, Maryland. Her sympathies were for the Union, and neither threats nor cajolery could move her to yield her flag to the Confederates. Finally she was permitted to wave her flag without interference. A poem was written about her by John Greenleaf Whittier.

FINISHING

Refer to the Backing Fabric and Batting instructions on page 103. Quilt as preferred, see the instructions on page 104, if needed. Refer to the Binding instructions on page 106.

Red Mountains

Red Mountains, 64" x 72". Made by Diana McClun and Laura Nownes; machine quilted by Kathy Sandbach.

PATTERN: Half-Square triangle

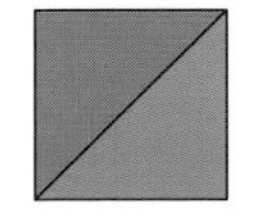

BLOCK SIZE: 4" finished

SETTING: Straight

TECHNIQUES: Quick-cutting and half-square triangles

FABRIC AND COLOR INSPIRATION: We wanted to make a red quilt.

To obtain this, we used a variety of red fabrics from light to dark and added yellow, yellow-green, orange, and blue to act as a background for the red peaks.

	Photo quilt	Queen	King
Finished size	64" x 72"	84" x 84"	100" x 92"
Blocks set	16 x 18	21 x 21	25 x 23
Number of Half-Square triangles	288	441	575

YARDAGE

Based on 42" wide fabric, from selvage to selvage

HALF-SQUARE TRIANGLES:			
Light, medium, and dark fabrics to total	5 1/4	8	10 1/4
Backing	4	7 1/2	8 1/4
Binding (1/4" finished)	1/2	5/8	3/4

CUTTING

Use Quick-cutting techniques on page 95.

HALF-SQUARE TRIANGLES:			
Number of 5" strips	36	56	72
Cut the strips into 5" squares. Then cut the squares in half diagonally.			
Backing: Piecing Diagram page 103	B	C	C

CONSTRUCTION

1. Sew light and dark triangles together to make Half-Square triangle blocks. Refer to page 27 for help, if needed.

2. A design wall is helpful for arranging the blocks before sewing. Refer to the photo quilt for placement.

HELPFUL HINT

Alternate the pressing direction of the seams at the intersections to eliminate bulk. It will be necessary to place a pin at each intersection to keep opposing seams close together and avoid slipping.

3. Sew the blocks together in vertical rows. Then sew the rows together in a straight setting.

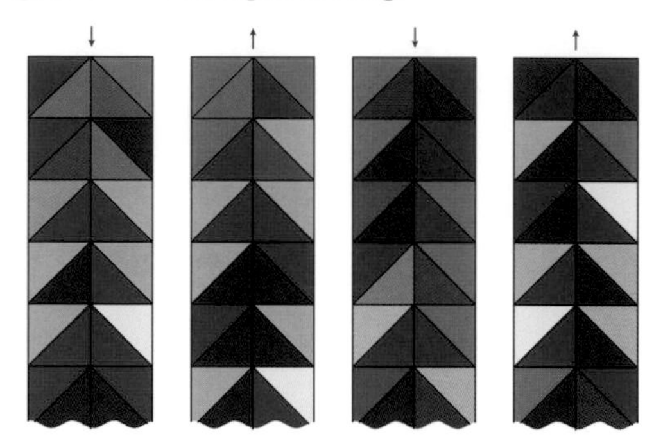

FINISHING

Refer to the Backing Fabric and Batting instructions on page 103. Quilt as preferred, see the instructions on page 104, if needed. Refer to the Binding instructions on page 106.

Stars and Leaves

Stars and Leaves, 65" x 65". Made by Diana McClun and Laura Nownes; machine quilted by Kathy Sandbach.

PATTERN: Half-Square triangle

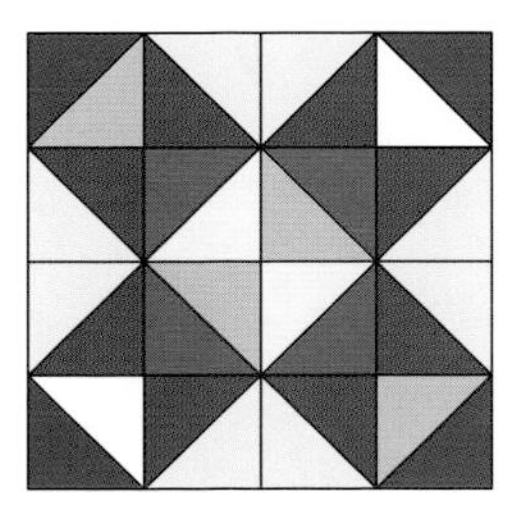

BLOCK SIZE: 16" finished

SETTING: Straight with sashing

TECHNIQUES: Quick-cutting and half-square triangle

FABRIC AND COLOR INSPIRATION: We chose a fall theme, using leaf print fabrics in the colors of autumn.

	Photo quilt	Double/Queen	King
Finished size	65" x 65"	$82\frac{1}{2}$" x $82\frac{1}{2}$"	100" x 100"
Blocks set	3 x 3	4 x 4	5 x 5
Number of blocks	9	16	25
Number of Half-Square triangles	144	256	400

YARDAGE

Based on 42" wide fabric, from selvage to selvage

	Photo quilt	Double/Queen	King
HALF-SQUARE TRIANGLES:			
Light, medium and dark fabrics to total	$2\frac{3}{4}$	$4\frac{3}{4}$	$7\frac{1}{4}$
Sashing and inner border			
Cut crosswise	1	$1\frac{1}{4}$	$1\frac{3}{4}$
Outer border			
Cut crosswise	$1\frac{1}{4}$	$1\frac{5}{8}$	2
or Cut lengthwise	2	$2\frac{3}{8}$	$2^{7}{}_{8}$
Backing	4	$7\frac{1}{4}$	9
Binding ($\frac{1}{4}$" finished)	$\frac{1}{2}$	$\frac{5}{8}$	$\frac{3}{4}$

CUTTING

Use Quick-cutting techniques on page 95.

	Photo quilt	Double/Queen	King
HALF-SQUARE TRIANGLES:			
Number of 5" strips	18	32	50
Cut into 5" squares. Cut the squares in half diagonally.			
Sashing and inner border:			
Number of 2" strips	12	20	28
Cut into 2" x $16\frac{1}{2}$" vertical sashing pieces	6	12	20
(Remaining strips will be used for horizontal sashing and inner border)			
Outer border:			
Cut crosswise			
Number of 6" strips	7	9	11
or Cut lengthwise			
Number of 6" strips	4	4	4
Backing: Piecing Diagram page 103	A	C	C

CONSTRUCTION

1. Sew light and dark triangles together to make the required number of Half-Square triangle blocks. Refer to page 27 for help, if needed.

2. To make each star block, lay out the Half-Square triangles, as shown.

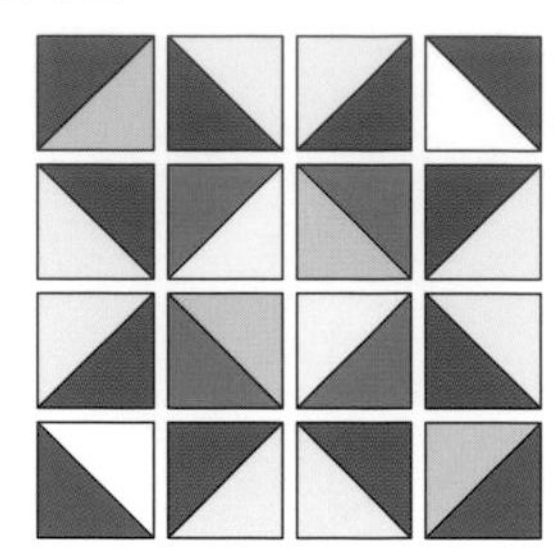

3. Sew the Half-Square triangles together in rows, with a continuous chain of thread joining the rows. Press the seam allowances in the opposite directions in each row.

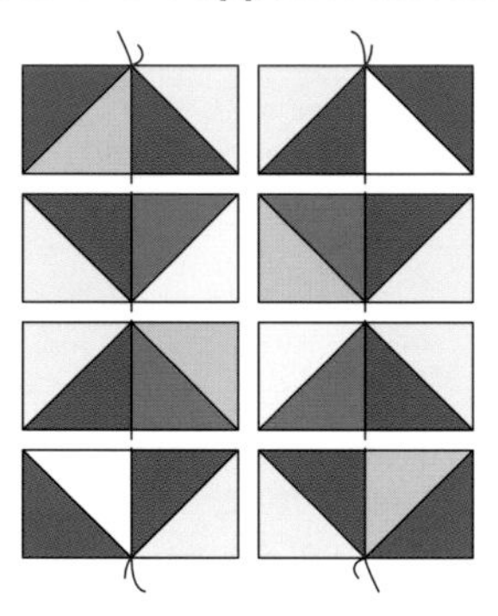

4. Sew the rows together. Press the seam allowances in the direction indicated by the arrows.

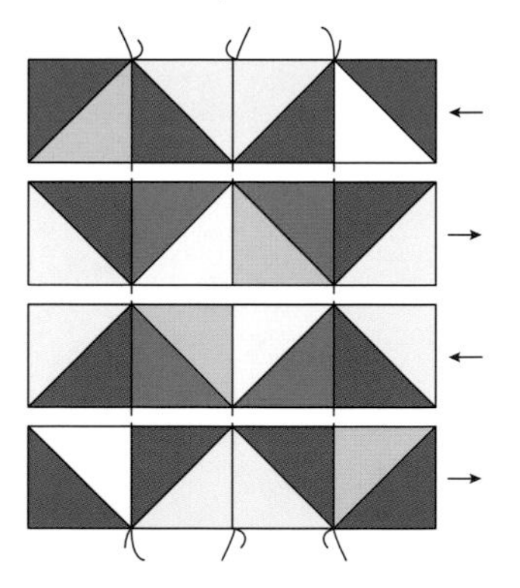

CHECKPOINT:
The star block should measure $16\frac{1}{2}$".

5. Sew the star blocks in rows with vertical sashing strips. Press the seams toward the sashing strips.

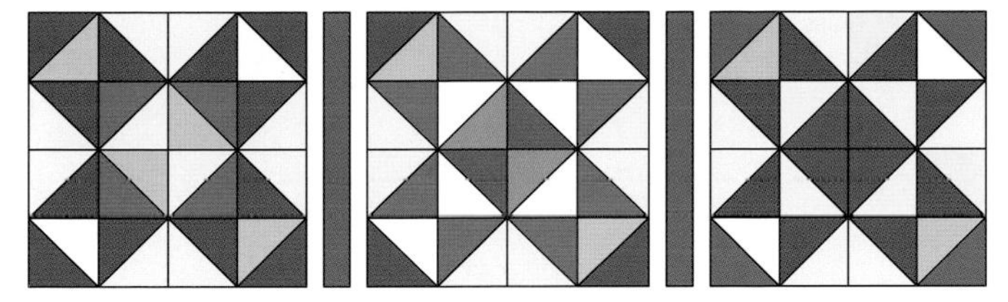

6. Piece the horizontal sashing strips together end to end to the lengths needed. Join the rows of blocks together with the horizontal sashing strips.

Helpful Hint

Place pins perpendicular, directly on the horizontal sashing, to mark the exact placement of the adjoining vertical sashing strips.

7. Attach the side inner borders, joining the strips end to end as needed. Then attach the top and bottom inner borders. Refer to page 102 for help, if needed.

8. Attach the side outer borders and then the top and bottom outer borders to complete the quilt top.

FINISHING

Refer to the Backing Fabric and Batting instructions on page 103. Quilt as preferred, see the instructions on page 104, if needed. Refer to the Binding instructions on page 106.

Love Rings

Love Rings, 56" x 56". Made by Diana McClun and Laura Nownes; machine quilted by Kathy Sandbach.

PATTERNS: Half-Square triangles

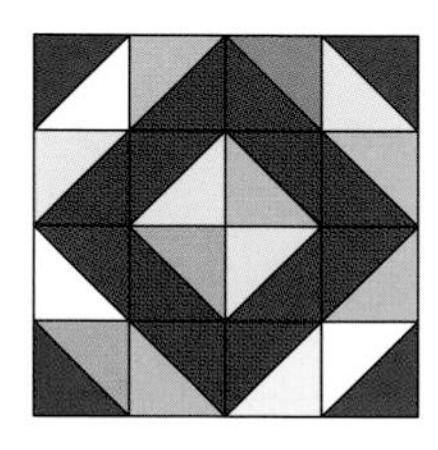

BLOCK SIZE: 16" finished

SETTING: Straight

TECHNIQUES: Quick-cutting, strip piecing, and half-square triangle

FABRIC AND COLOR INSPIRATION:

The fabric collection "Tropical Fling" designed by Susie Robbins for P&B Textiles was the inspiration. These romantic, realistic floral prints are combined with grayed and soft pastels, and accented with white.

	Photo Quilt	Queen	King
Finished size	56" x 56"	88" x 88"	104" x 104"
Blocks set	3 x 3	5 x 5	6 x 6
Total number of blocks	9	25	36
Total Half-Square triangles	144	400	576

YARDAGE

Based on 42" fabric, from selvage to selvage

HALF-SQUARE TRIANGLES:			
Light and dark fabrics			
each to total	1 1/2	3 5/8	5 1/4
FENCE:			
Light fabric (includes railing)	1	1 3/8	1 1/2
Dark fabrics to total	5/8	7/8	1
Backing	3 1/2	7 3/4	9 1/4
Binding (1/4" finished)	1/2	5/8	3/4

CUTTING

Use Quick-cutting techniques on page 95.

HALF-SQUARE TRIANGLES:			
Light and dark fabrics:			
Number of 5" strips **each**	9	25	36

Cut strips into 5" squares. Then cut the squares in half diagonally.

FENCE:			
Light: 1 1/2" strips (includes railing)	15	25	30
Darks: 1 1/2" strips	9	15	18
Backing: Piecing Diagram page 103	A	C	C

CONSTRUCTION

1. Make the required number of Half-Square triangles. Refer to the instructions on page 27 for help, if needed.

2. Arrange the Half-Square triangles as shown. Sew into rows. Then sew the rows.

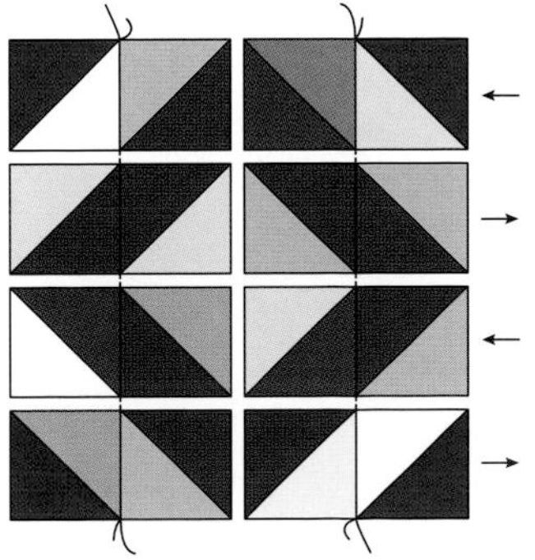

3. Sew the blocks together, alternating the direction of the seams at the intersections, if possible. If not, use pins to secure the seams and prevent them from shifting while sewing. Carefully press on the wrong and then the right side.

4. Sew the light and dark strips together to make the Fence sets. Refer to the instructions on page 17 for help, if needed.

5. Join enough fence units to equal the length of the quilt sides. Attach railing strips to the fences, seaming as necessary. Refer to instructions on page 17 for help, if needed. Attach the fence strips to the sides of the quilt.

NOTE

The fence railing is 1" finished in this quilt.

6. Construct and then attach the top and bottom fence to the railing using the same technique described above. Attach the top and bottom fence strips to the quilt.

FINISHING

Refer to the Backing Fabric and Batting instructions on page 103. Quilt as preferred, see the instructions on page 104, if needed. Refer to the Binding instructions on page 106.

CHAPTER 4

Quarter-Square Triangles

Quarter-Square Triangles

6" block

The term Quarter-Square triangle can refer to an individual triangle or multiple triangles of the same size sewn together. As a block, the Quarter-Square triangle consists of four triangles sewn together to form a square. The difference between these triangles and the Half-Square triangles is the cutting. It is always best to have the straight grain of the fabric along the outer edges of a block (or quilt top). When projects instruct cutting squares into quarters diagonally, this is why it is done.

BLOCK SIZE: 6" finished
SHAPE: Triangle
TECHNIQUES: Quick-cutting and quarter-square triangles
FABRIC SUGGESTIONS: One or more fabrics can be used.

How to make Quarter-Square Triangles

YARDAGE

To make ten blocks:

1/4 yard **each** of two fabrics, one light and one dark

CUTTING

Light and dark fabric:

Cut one 7 1/4" strip of **each** fabric.

Cut the strips into 7 1/4" squares.

Cut the squares into quarters diagonally as shown.

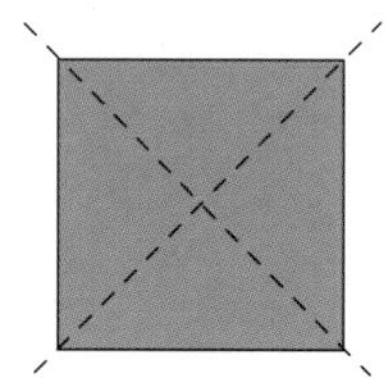

CONSTRUCTION

1. Place a light and dark triangle with their right sides together and edges even with each other.

2. Starting at the corner, stitch the triangles together.

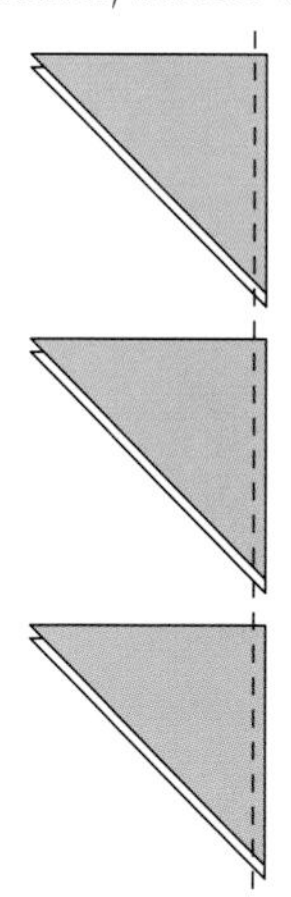

HELPFUL HINT

Several pairs of triangles can be sewn together in a "chain" leaving a few stitches between units, as shown. Be consistent in placing either the light or dark triangle on top when sewing. Be careful not to pull or stretch these edges, since they are cut along the bias.

3. Cut the chained units apart.

4. With the wrong side of the darker triangle on top, place the unit onto the pressing board. Press the seam allowance flat on the wrong side. Then carefully lift the darker triangle to open the unit and press over the seam allowance, in the direction indicated by the arrow.

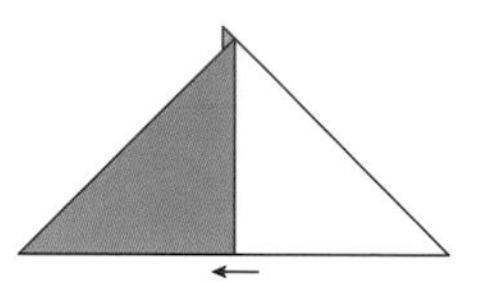

5. Place two units right sides together and secure with pins at the intersection. Carefully stitch the units together to complete the block.

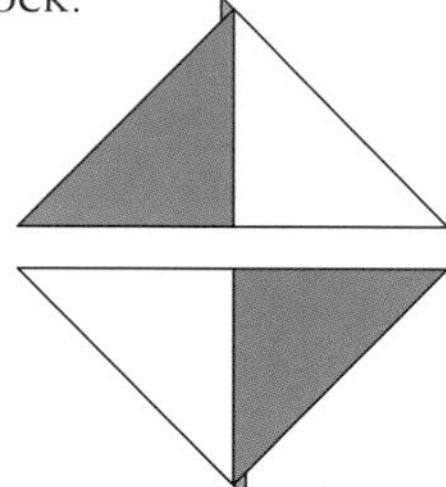

6. Press the seam flat on the wrong side first, and then to one side.

7. Place the block onto the cutting board. Place a ruler over the block with the marked 45° angle line over a seam, and the corner directly over the corner of the block. Use the cutting tools to trim each corner extension.

✔ CHECKPOINT:

The block should measure 6 1/2" square. Trim if necessary, being careful to keep the seams accurately meeting at each corner.

These simple representational patterns help to tell a story and set a scene when used within a quilt.

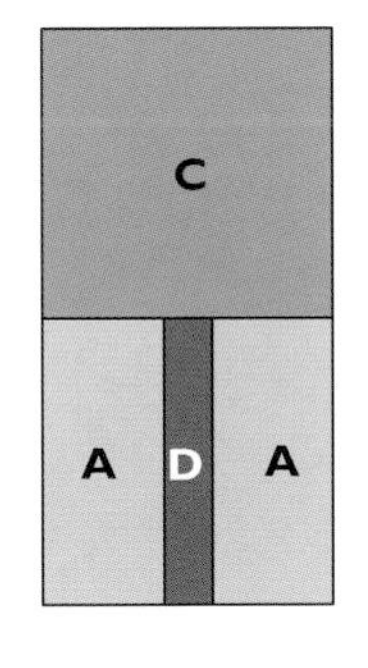

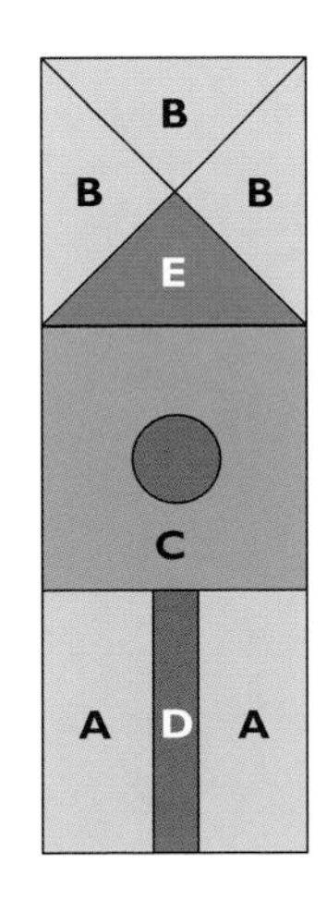

PATTERNS: Birdhouse (and Tree variation)

TREE BLOCK SIZE: 6" x 12" finished

BIRDHOUSE BLOCK SIZE: 6" x varying lengths as needed for individual quilts

SHAPES: Squares, Rectangles, and Quarter-Square triangles

TECHNIQUES: Quick-cutting, strip piecing, quarter-square triangles, and appliqué

FABRIC SUGGESTIONS: Tree: One each for sky, tree top, and trunk Birdhouse: One each for sky, roof, birdhouse, circle, and pole

How to make a Tree and a Birdhouse

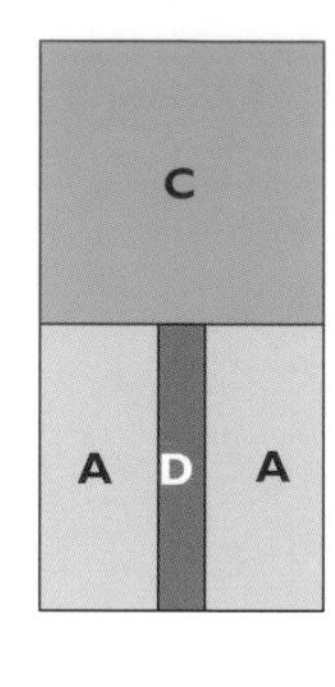

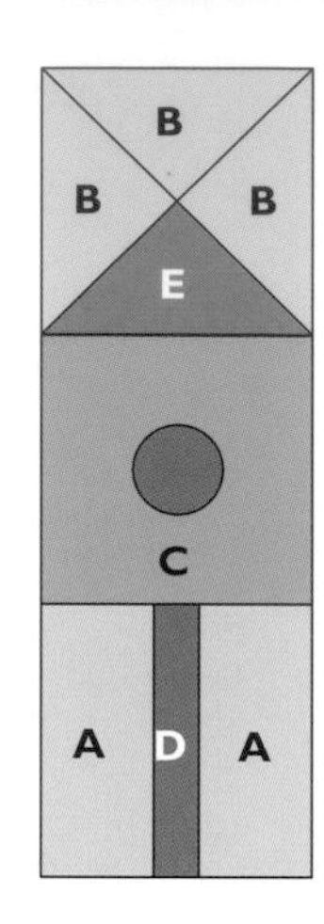

YARDAGE

Tree: 1/4 yard **each** of two fabrics (sky and tree), 1/8 yard for trunk

Birdhouse: 1/4 yard **each** of three fabrics (sky, roof, and house) 1/8 yard **each** of two fabrics (pole and circle)

CUTTING

To make one block of **each**:

Sky (A): Cut two 3" x 6 1/2" pieces. These lengths may vary with individual projects.

Birdhouse only (B): Cut one 7 1/4" square. Cut the square into quarters diagonally, as shown. You will need three of the four triangles.

Tree top or House (C): Cut one 6 1/2" square.

Trunk/Pole (D): Cut one 1 1/2" x 6 1/2" piece. This length may vary with individual projects.

Roof (E): Cut one 7 1/4" square.

Cut the square into quarters diagonally, as shown. You will need only one of the four triangles.

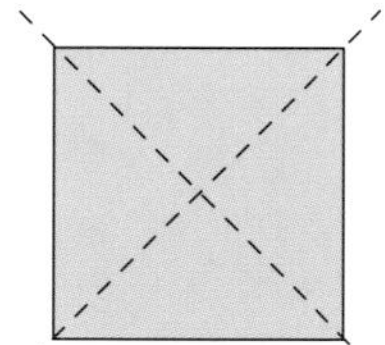

Circle: For Birdhouse, use small circle pattern on page 108.

CONSTRUCTION

1. Sew sky (A) and trunk or pole (D) together. Press the seams in the direction indicated by the arrows.

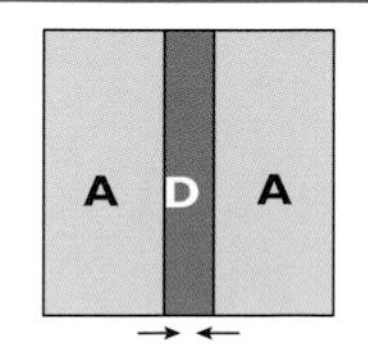

HELPFUL HINT

If making several blocks using the same fabrics, sew longer strips together then cut them apart every 6 1/2", as shown. This measurement will vary with individual projects.

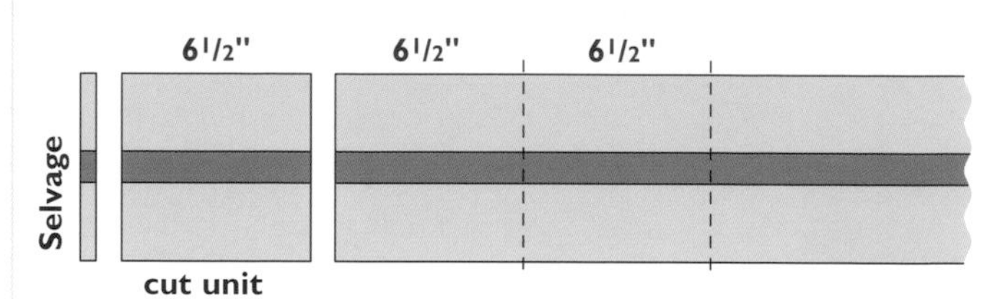

2. Sew the tree top or house (C) to the sky/trunk unit. Press the seam in the direction indicated by the arrow. This completes the tree block. Continue with the following steps to complete the birdhouse.

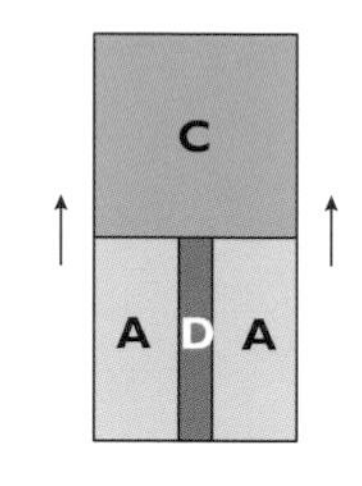

3. Sew the roof (E) to a sky triangle (B). Press in the direction indicated by the arrow. These units are called quarter-square triangles.

4. Sew the two remaining sky triangles (B) together. Press in the direction indicated by the arrow.

5. Sew the sky and roof units together, as shown.

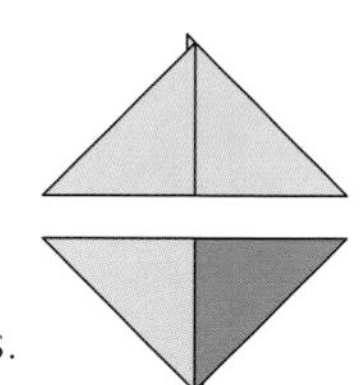

CHECKPOINT:

The unit should measure 6 1/2".
If necessary, trim and straighten the edges.

6. Attach the sky/roof unit to the top of the birdhouse unit to complete the Birdhouse block. Press in the direction indicated by the arrows.

7. Trace and cut a plastic template using the small circle pattern on page 108. Add the circle to the birdhouse using your preferred method of appliqué, referring to page 98 for help, if needed.

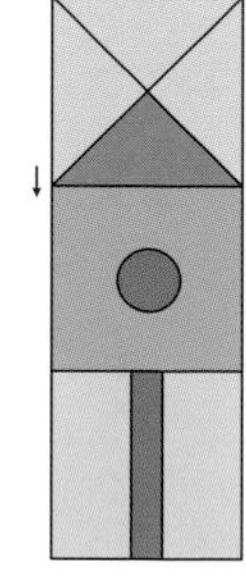

Birds Return

Birds Return, 45" x 57". Made by Diana McClun and Laura Nownes; machine quilted by Kathy Sandbach.

PATTERNS: Birdhouse and Appliquéd bird

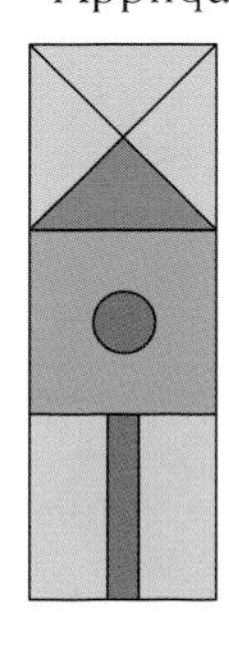

BLOCK SIZE: 6" x 21" finished

ALTERNATE BLOCKS: 6" square finished and 3" x 6" finished

SETTING: Straight, vertical rows using the alternate blocks as a half-step

TECHNIQUES: Quick-cutting, strip piecing, and appliqué.

FABRIC AND COLOR INSPIRATION: A cat and bird printed fabric was the inspiration. Although this fabric was never used in the quilt, the colors were selected from the fabric using a complimentary color scheme of red-orange and blue-green, with black and white as the accents. A wide range of sky prints was used for the backgrounds.

	Photo Quilt
Finished size	45" x 57"
Number of birdhouse blocks	15

YARDAGE

Based on 42" wide fabric, from selvage to selvage

BIRDHOUSE BLOCKS:	
Sky fabrics to total	1 1/2
Roof fabrics to total	1/4
House fabrics to total	3/4
Poles	1/4
Circles	1/4
Birds fabrics to total	3/8
Alternate blocks: fabrics to total	5/8
Borders cut crosswise	3/8
Backing	3
Binding (1/4" finished)	3/8

CUTTING

Use Quick-cutting techniques on page 95.

BIRDHOUSE BLOCKS:	
Sky: number of 7 1/4" squares	15
Cut squares into quarters diagonally.	
Number of 3" strips	8
Roofs: number of 7 1/4" squares	4
Cut the squares into quarters diagonally.	
Houses: number of 6 1/2"strips	3
Cut the strips into 6 1/2" squares.	
Poles: number of 1 1/2" strips	4
Circles: (use pattern on page 108)	12
(Some houses in the photo do not have circles)	
Birds: (use pattern on page 108)	10
Alternate blocks:	
Number of 6 1/2" strips	3
Then cut into 3 1/2" x 6 1/2" rectangles	4
and 6 1/2" squares.	10
Border: number of 2" strips	5
Backing: Piecing Diagram page 103	A

CONSTRUCTION

1. Make the required number of Birdhouse blocks. Refer to the instructions on page 44 for help, if needed.

NOTE

For this project, the pieces for the sky/pole unit are 9 1/2" long and one birdhouse does not have the sky/pole unit.

2. A design wall is helpful in arranging the birdhouse blocks and alternate blocks. Refer to the diagram below for placement of the blocks and alternate blocks.

3. Sew the birdhouse and alternate blocks together in vertical rows. Then sew the rows together.

4. Add the birds to the quilt using your preferred method of appliqué, referring to the instructions on page 98 for help, if needed.

5. Sew the border strips together end to end and cut the length needed. Attach the borders to the sides and then to the top and bottom to complete the quilt top. Refer to page 102 for help, if needed.

FINISHING

Refer to the Backing Fabric and Batting instructions on page 103. Quilt as preferred, or see the instructions on page 104, if needed. Refer to the Binding instructions on page 106.

CHAPTER 5

Square-in-a-Square Block

Square-in-a-Square Block

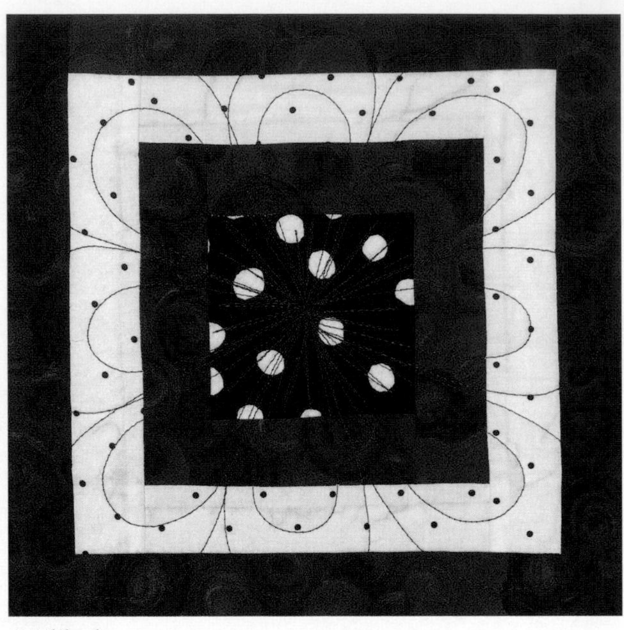

9" block

This is a simple variation of the traditional Log Cabin block.

BLOCK SIZE: 9" finished

SHAPES: Squares and rectangles

TECHNIQUES: Quick-cutting

FABRIC SUGGESTIONS: Three fabrics: one for center, one **each** light fabric and dark fabric for strips.

How to make a Square-in-a-Square

YARDAGE

To make four blocks:

Center: $^1/_8$ yard

Light fabric strips: $^1/_4$ yard

Dark fabric strips: $^3/_8$ yard

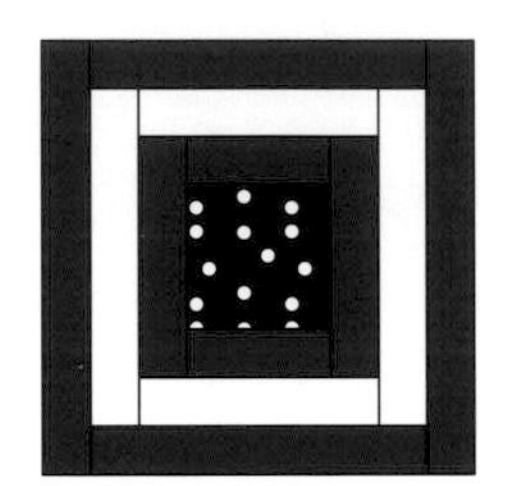

CUTTING

Center: Cut one $3^1/_2$" strip.
Cut into four $3^1/_2$" squares.

Light fabric strips: Cut three $1^1/_2$" strips.

Dark fabric strips: Cut six $1^1/_2$" strips.

CONSTRUCTION

1. With the right sides together, sew the center squares to a dark strip.

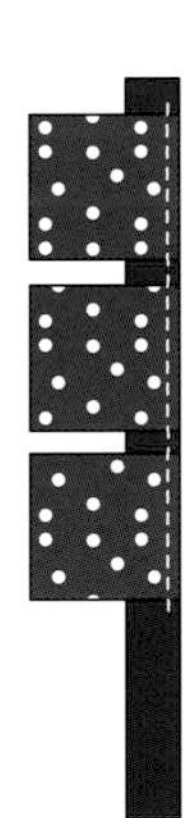

2. Press the seams first on the wrong side, then on the right side in the direction indicated by the arrows.

3. Cut the units apart.

CHECKPOINT
The new units should measure 3 1/2" x 4 1/2". Trim to the needed size, if necessary.

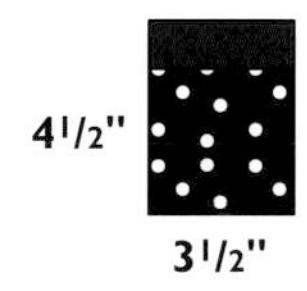

4. With the right sides together, place the units onto a dark strip and sew as shown.

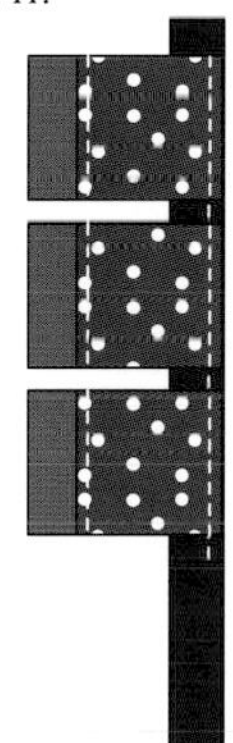

5. Press the seams first on the wrong side, then on the right side in the direction indicated by the arrows.

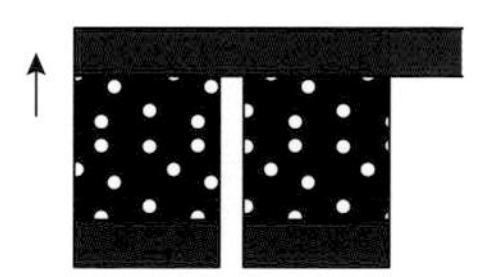

6. Cut the units apart.

CHECKPOINT
The new units should measure 3 1/2" x 5 1/2". Trim to the needed size, if necessary.

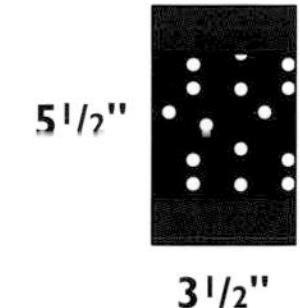

7. With the right sides together, place the units onto a dark strip and sew.

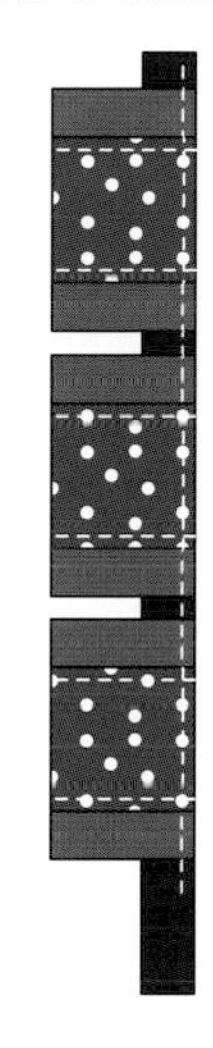

8. Press the seam away from the center square as before and cut the units apart.

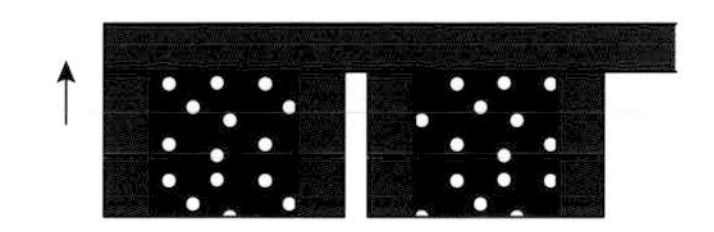

CHECKPOINT
The new units should measure 4 1/2" x 5 1/2". Trim to the needed size, if necessary.

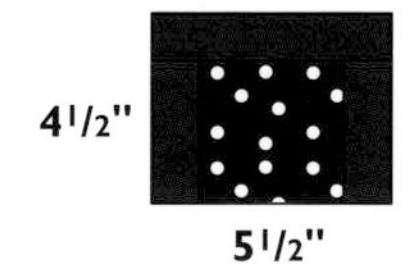

9. With the right sides together, place the units onto a dark strip and sew.

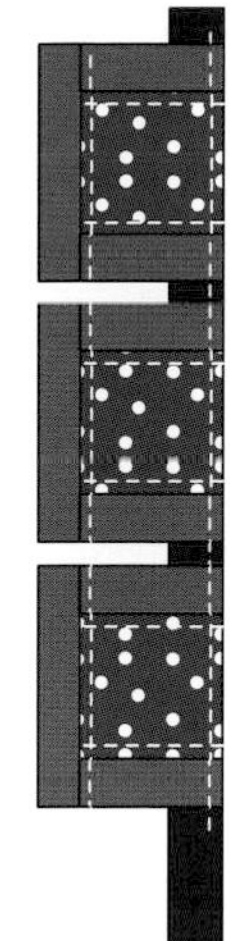

10. Press the strip away from the center and cut the units apart, as shown.

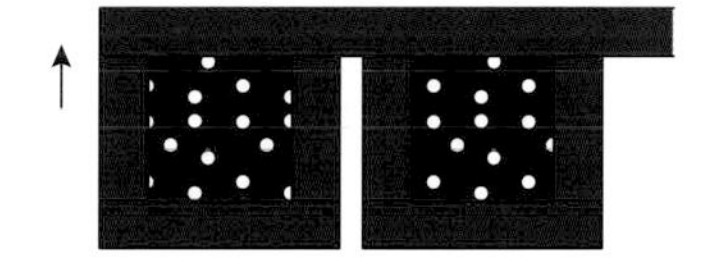

CHECKPOINT
The new units should measure 5 1/2" x 5 1/2". Trim if needed.

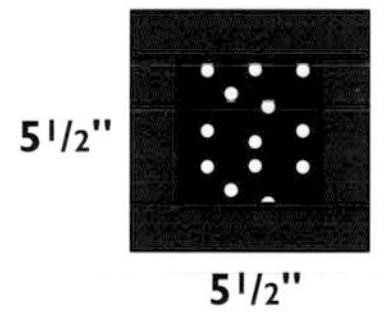

11. Repeat Steps 1 through 10, to add the light and then the remaining dark strips.

CHECKPOINT
The completed blocks should measure 9 1/2" x 9 1/2".

Basket Block

12" block

The Basket block is a variation of the Square-in-a-Square block.

BLOCK SIZE: 12" finished
SHAPES: Squares, Rectangles, and Quarter-Square triangles
TECHNIQUES: Quick-cutting and quarter-square triangles
FABRIC SUGGESTIONS: One fabric for the background, one for the center of the basket, one for the base, and two contrasting fabrics for the strips.

How to make a Basket

YARDAGE

To make four Basket blocks:
Background: $^5/_8$ yard
Base: $^1/_4$ yard
Center: $^1/_8$ yard
Light fabric: $^1/_8$ yard
Dark fabric: $^1/_4$ yard

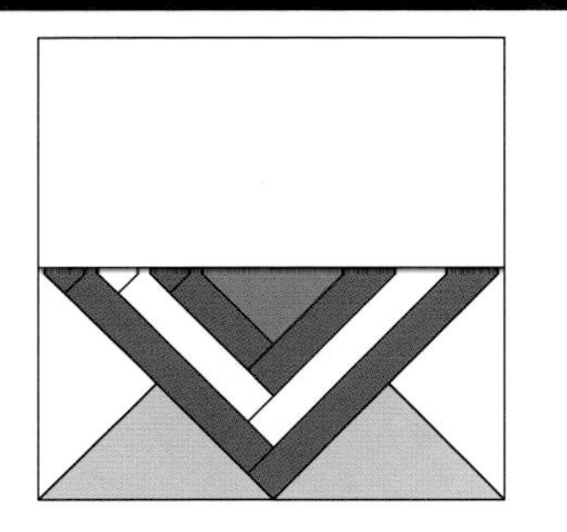

CUTTING

Center: Cut two $3^1/_2$" squares.
Light fabric strips: Cut two $1^1/_2$" strips.
Dark fabric strips: Cut three $1^1/_2$" strips.
Background:
Cut one $12^1/_2$" strip.
Cut strip into four $6\,^1/_2$" x $12^1/_2$" rectangles.
Cut one $7\,^1/_4$" square
Cut the square into quarters diagonally.
Base:
Cut two $7\,^1/_4$" squares.
Cut the squares into quarters diagonally.

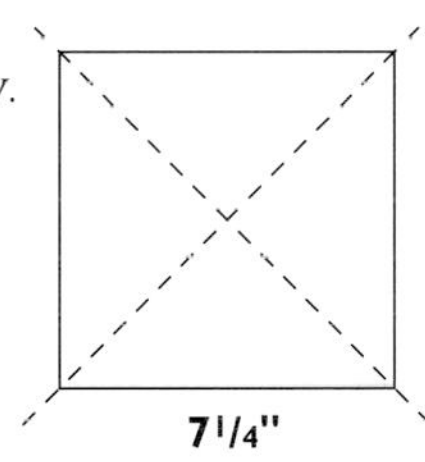

CONSTRUCTION

1. Follow Steps 1-11 for making the Square-in-a-Square block on page 48.

2. Carefully cut the blocks in half diagonally as you would for Half-Square triangles. The blocks are very fragile and will easily stretch along the bias edge. Handle them as little as possible.

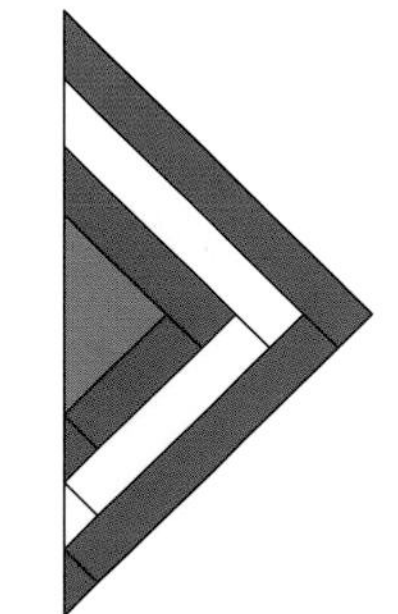

3. Make the base units, sewing the background and base triangles together. Press in the direction indicated by the arrows.

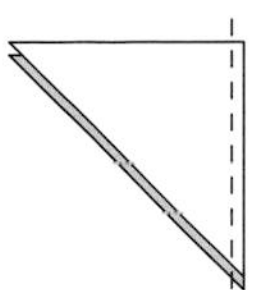

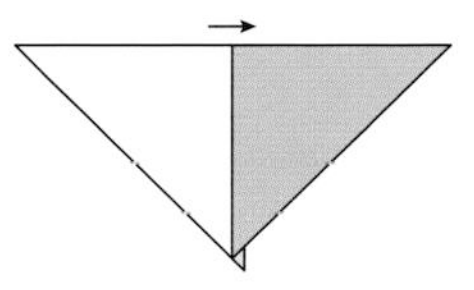

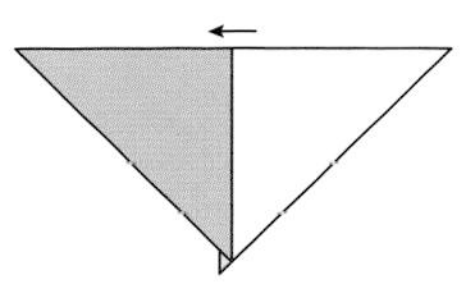

4. Sew the left and right base units to the basket. Be sure that there is a $^1/_4$" extension of base fabric beyond the bottom edge of the basket. Press the seams toward the basket, as indicated by the arrows.

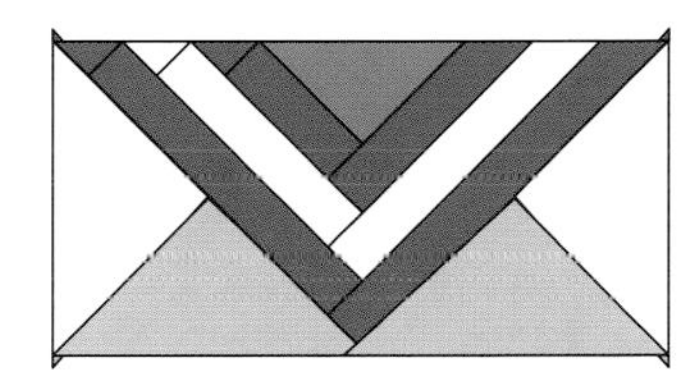

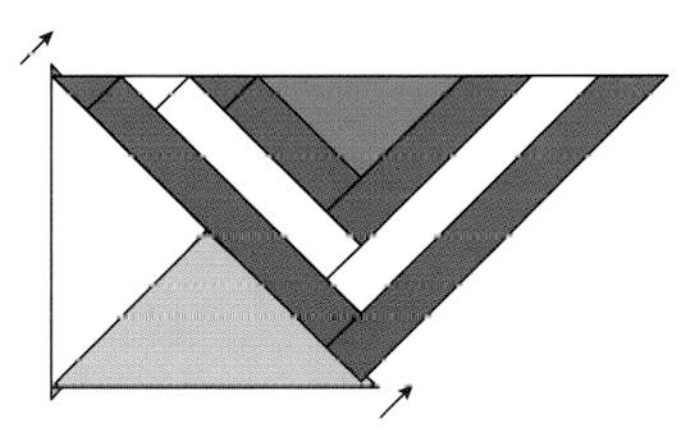

CHECKPOINT:
The bottom half of the block should measure $6^1/_2$" x $12^1/_2$". Trim if necessary.

5. Sew the $6^1/_2$" x $12^1/_2$" background rectangle to the top of the basket. Press the seam toward the background.

HELPFUL HINT
To eliminate the stretching which can occur along the top edge of the basket bottom, place the top background piece onto the basket bottom, right side together. Pin at opposite ends. Carefully press flat. Place additional pins along the edges, then sew.

CHECKPOINT:
The completed block should measure $12^1/_2$" x $12^1/_2$".

Winter Flowers

Winter Flowers, 64" x 73". Made by Diana McClun and Laura Nownes; machine quilted by Kathy Sandbach.

PATTERN: Square-in-a-Square

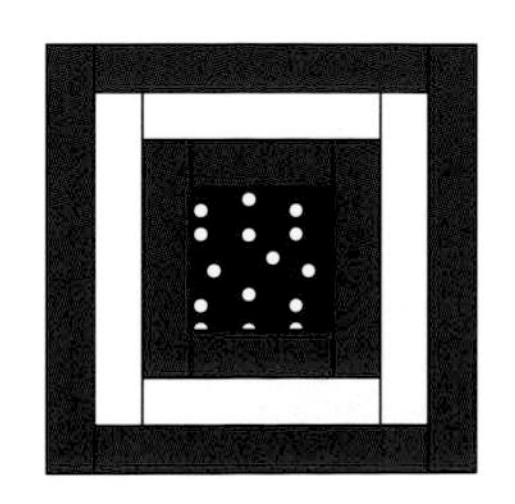

BLOCK SIZE: 9" finished

ALTERNATE BLOCKS: 4½" x 9" finished

SETTING: Straight in vertical rows using the alternate block as a half-step.

TECHNIQUES: Quick-cutting

FABRIC AND COLOR INSPIRATION:
The large floral border fabric was the springboard for the black and white. Gold, purple, and red were added to represent the flowers within the blocks. The fabrics with music and bare branches enhance the winter theme.

	Photo quilt	Queen	King
Finished size	64" x 73"	82" x 86 1/2"	100" x 100"
Blocks set	5 x 4	7 x 5	9 x 6
Number of Square-in-a-Square blocks	20	35	54
Number of alternate blocks	20	35	54

YARDAGE

Based on 42" wide fabric, from selvage to selvage

	Photo quilt	Queen	King
SQUARE-IN-A-SQUARE BLOCKS:			
Center fabrics (two) **each**	1/4	1/4	3/8
Light fabric	3/4	1 1/8	1 3/4
Dark fabrics (two) **each**	3/4	1 1/8	1 3/4
ALTERNATE BLOCKS:			
Five fabrics **each**	3/8	3/8	1/2
Inner Border:			
Cut crosswise	1/2	5/8	3/4
Outer border:			
Cut crosswise	1 3/4	2	2 1/2
or Cut lengthwise	2 1/8	2 1/2	3
Backing	4	7 1/4	9
Binding (1/4" finished)	1/2	5/8	3/4

CUTTING

Use Quick-cutting techniques on page 95.

	Photo quilt	Queen	King
SQUARE-IN-A-SQUARE BLOCKS:			
Centers: Number of 3 1/2" strips from **each** fabric	1	2	3
Light fabric: Number of 1 1/2" strips	14	24	38
Dark fabrics: Number of 1 1/2" strips from **each** fabric	14	25	38
ALTERNATE BLOCKS:			
Number of 5" strips from **each**	2	2	3
Cut strips into 5" x 9 1/2" pieces.			
Inner border:			
Number of 2 1/2" strips	6	7	9
Outer border:			
Cut crosswise: number of 8" strips	7	8	11
or Cut lengthwise: Number of 8" strips	4	4	4
Backing: Piecing Diagram page 103	A	D	C

CONSTRUCTION

1. Make the required number of Square-in-a-Square blocks. Refer to the instructions on page 48 for help, if needed.

2. A design wall is very helpful when arranging blocks. Refer to photo for placement of the blocks.

3. Sew the blocks together in vertical rows and then sew the rows together. Refer to the instructions on page 101 for help, if needed.

4. Attach the top and bottom inner borders and then the side inner borders. Attach the outer borders in the same manner to complete the quilt top. Refer to the instructions on page 102 for help, if needed.

FINISHING

Refer to the Backing Fabric and Batting instructions on page 103. Quilt as preferred, see the instructions on page 104, if needed. Refer to the Binding instructions on page 106.

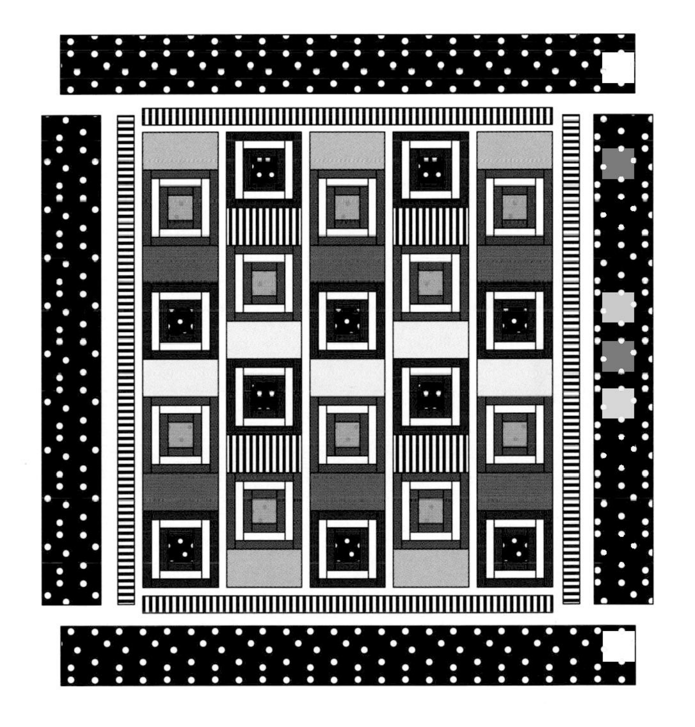

From Me to You

From Me to You, 64" x 77". Made by Diana McClun and Christine Sutton; machine quilted by Kathy Sandbach.

PATTERN: Square-in-a-Square

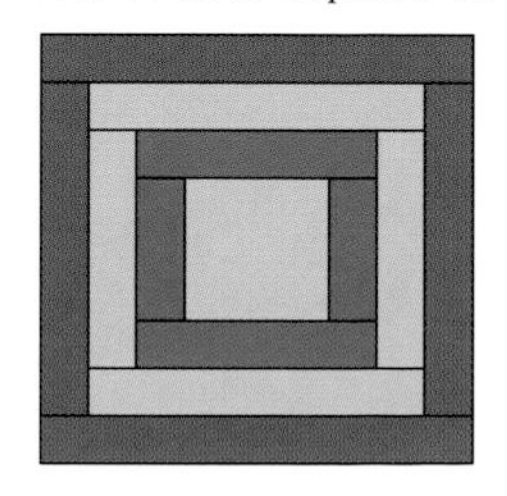

BLOCK SIZE: 9" finished

SETTING: Diagonal

TECHNIQUES: Quick-cutting

FABRIC AND COLOR INSPIRATION:
Invite a friend to come and choose from your stash. Let her add some of her own pieces using the full color spectrum. The mood and many flowers that grow in the garden give organization to the colors. The blue sky is used as the background.

	Photo Quilt	Queen	King
Finished size	64" x 77"	90" x 90"	103" x 103"
Blocks set	5 x 6	7 x 7	8 x 8
Number of blocks	50	85	113

Helpful Hint

To achieve the same look as in the photo, a variety of fabrics is required. Use scraps from your stash, or if you choose to purchase fabric, requirements for each combination are listed below.

YARDAGE

Based on 42" wide fabric, from selvage to selvage

SQUARE-IN-A-SQUARE BLOCKS:			
Number of Combinations:	13	22	29
(Three to four fabrics each)			
For **each** combination			
Center	1/8	1/8	1/8
Other fabrics to total	1/2	1/2	1/2
Setting triangles	1 1/2	1 1/2	1 3/4
Backing	4	8	9
Binding (1/4" finished)	1/2	5/8	3/4

CUTTING

Use Quick-cutting techniques on page 95.

SQUARE-IN-A-SQUARE BLOCKS:			
For **each** combination:			
Center:			
Number of 3 1/2" strips	1	1	1
Cut strips into 3 1/2" squares.			
Number of 1 1/2" strips	9	9	9
Side setting triangles:			
Number of 15" strips	3	3	4
Cut into 15" squares.	5	6	7
Cut the squares into quarters diagonally.			
Corner setting triangles: Number of 10 1/2" squares			
Cut in half diagonally.	2	2	2
Backing: Piecing Diagram page 103	B	C	C

CONSTRUCTION

1. Make the required total number of Square-in-a-Square blocks. Refer to page 48 for help, if needed.

2. Arrange all of the blocks, side and corner triangles in your desired arrangement. A design wall is helpful to determine placement.

3. Sew the blocks together with the setting triangles in diagonal rows. Refer to the instructions for diagonal set on page 102 for help, if needed.

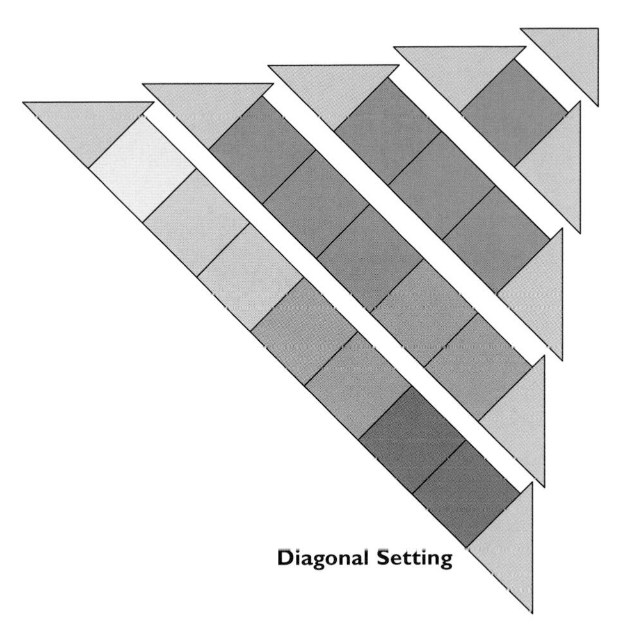

Diagonal Setting

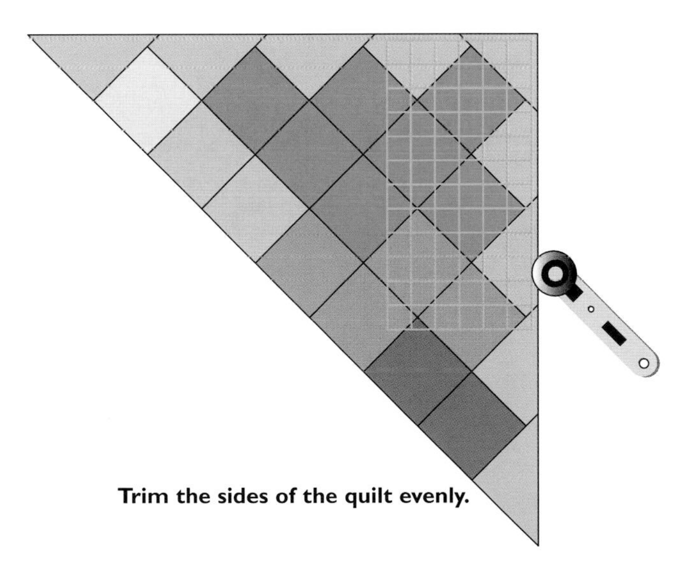

Trim the sides of the quilt evenly.

FINISHING

Refer to the Backing Fabric and Batting instructions on page 103. Quilt as preferred, see the instructions on page 104, if needed. Refer to the Binding instructions on page 106.

Apple Time

Apple Time, 69" x 69". Made by Diana McClun and Laura Nownes; machine quilted by Kathy Sandbach.

PATTERN: Square-in-a-Square

BLOCK SIZE: 12" finished
SETTING: Straight
TECHNIQUES: Quick-cutting and appliqué

FABRIC AND COLOR INSPIRATION: Fabrics in many shades of neutrals, from beige to brown, were used to interpret the basket theme. Several shades of red and green were used for the apples and leaves.

	Photo Quilt	Queen	King
Finished size	69" x 69"	93" x 93"	105" x 105"
Blocks set	5 x 5	7 x 7	8 x 8
Number of blocks	25	49	64
Number of Square-in-a-Square blocks	13	25	32

YARDAGE

Based on 42" wide fabric, from selvage to selvage

	Photo Quilt	Queen	King
BASKETS:			
Centers	3/8	1/2	1/2
Light background fabrics: three **each**	1	1 3/4	2
Medium fabrics (includes bases)	1 1/4	2	2 1/2
Dark fabrics	1 1/4	1 3/4	2 1/4
Apples: fabrics to total	1	1 5/8	2 1/8
Leaves: fabrics to total	1/4	1/2	3/4
Border: Light fabric	1/2	5/8	3/4
Dark fabric	7/8	1 1/4	1 1/2
Backing	4 1/4	8 1/4	9 3/8
Binding (1/4" finished)	1/2	5/8	3/4

CUTTING

Use Quick-cutting techniques on page 95.

	Photo Quilt	Queen	King
BASKETS:			
Light background fabrics:			
Number of 12 1/2" strips	5	9	11
Cut strips into 6 1/2" x 12 1/2" pieces.	25	49	64
Number of 7 1/4" strips	3	5	7
Cut strips into 7 1/4" squares.	13	25	32
Cut the squares into quarters diagonally.			
Centers:			
Number of 3 1/2" strips	2	3	3
Number of 3 1/2" squares	13	25	32
Number of 1 1/2" strips	9	17	21
Number of 7 1/4" strips	3	5	7
Bases:			
Cut strips into 7 1/4" squares.	13	25	32
Cut the squares into quarters diagonally.			
Dark fabrics: Number of 1 1/2" strips	18	34	43
Border: Number of 2" strips			
Light fabric	7	10	11
Dark fabric	13	18	21

	Photo Quilt	Queen	King
Apples (use pattern on page 109)	100	196	256
Leaves (use pattern on page 109)	25	49	64
Backing: Piecing Diagram page 103	B	C	C

CONSTRUCTION

1. Make the required number of Square-in-a-Square blocks. Refer to page 48 for help, if needed.

2. Cut the Square-in-a-Square blocks in half diagonally to make the half blocks required for the Baskets.

3. Make the required number of basket blocks. Refer to instructions on page 51 for help, if needed.

4. Use your preferred method of appliqué to attach the apples and leaves to the baskets. Trace the patterns on page 109 to make templates to cut 3-5 apples per block and one double leaf per block.

5. Refer to the photo quilt or the diagrams on page 58 for the placement of the Basket blocks. Sew the blocks together in a straight setting.

6. To make the border, sew enough light strips together end to end and cut to the length needed. Repeat with dark strips.

Helpful Hint

Due to the length of the border strips, it is best to first cut each strip to the exact needed length. This is determined by measuring both sides of the quilt top and through the center. Then, using an average, join the strips together in sets. This will prevent the set of strips from becoming wavy.

7. Sew the light and dark pieced strips together to make four border sets. Press the seams toward the dark strips.

8. Use the remaining light and dark strips to make two sets for the Nine-Patch corner blocks, as shown. Cut the sets apart every 2".

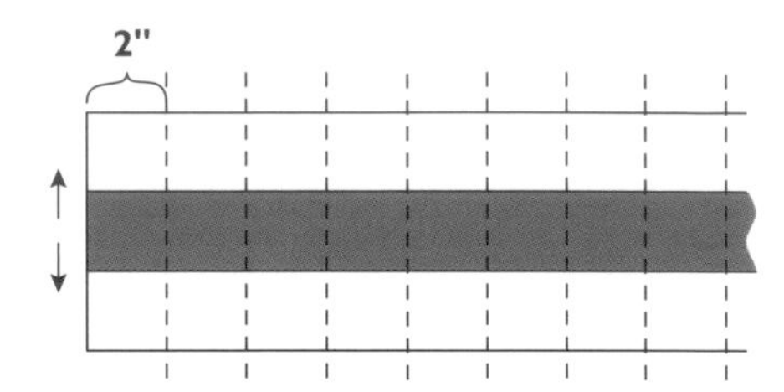

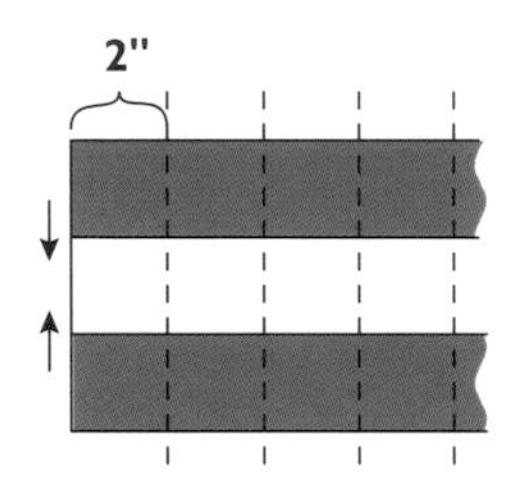

9. Sew the new pieced units together to make the four Nine-Patch corner blocks. Refer to instructions on page 15 for help, if needed.

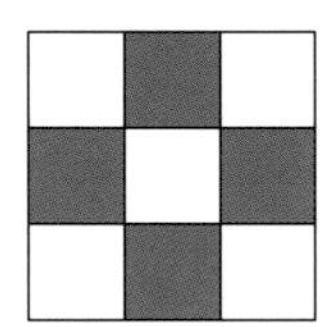

10. Sew two of the pieced borders to opposite sides of the quilt top.

11. Sew the corner blocks to each end of the two remaining pieced borders. Then sew them to the top and bottom to complete the quilt top.

FINISHING

Refer to the Backing Fabric and Batting instructions on page 103. Quilt as preferred, see the instructions on page 104, if needed. Refer to the Binding instructions on page 106.

Queen Size

King Size

Four Block Basket

Four Block Basket, 48" x 42". Made by Diana McClun and Laura Nownes; machine quilted by Kathy Sandbach.

PATTERN: Basket

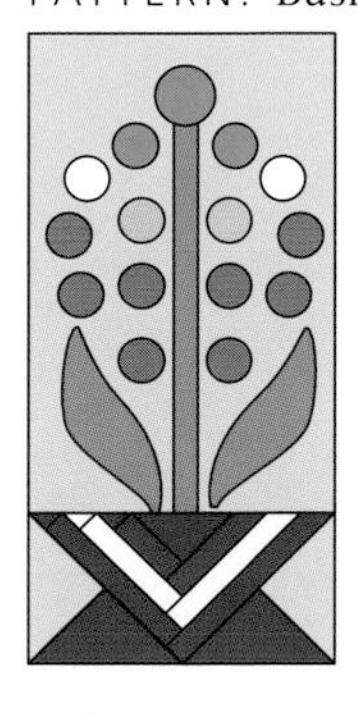

BLOCK SIZE: 12" x 24" finished
SETTING: Straight in horizontal rows
TECHNIQUES: Quick-cutting and appliqué

FABRIC AND COLOR INSPIRATION: Using various backgrounds for the same appliqué design adds interest to the repetition of the pattern. Borders add dimension. The large floral brings the flower border up close and the small flowers show well in the distance.

Finished size	48" x 42"
Number of Square-in-a-Square blocks	2

YARDAGE

Based on 42" wide fabric, from selvage to selvage

BASKET:	
Centers:	1/8
Light fabric	1/8
Dark fabric	1/2
Circles: fabrics to total	3/8
Backgrounds: fabrics to total	1/4
Leaves	3/8
Stems	1/4
Top inner border: Cut crosswise	1/4
Top outer border: Cut crosswise	3/8
Bottom inner border: Cut crosswise	3/8
Bottom outer border: Cut crosswise	5/8
Backing	2 5/8
Binding (1/4" finished)	3/8

CUTTING

Use Quick-cutting techniques on page 95.

Backgrounds: Number of 12 1/2" x 18 1/2" rectangles from **each** of four fabrics	1
Number of 7 1/4" squares from **each** of four fabrics. Cut squares into quarters diagonally.	1
BASKETS:	
Centers: Number of 3 1/2" squares	2
Light fabrics: Number of 1 1/2" strips	2
Dark fabrics: Number of 1 1/2" strips	3
Bases: Number of 7 1/4" squares. Cut squares into quarters diagonally	2
Stems: Number of 2 1/4" x 16 1/2" strips	4
Circles: (use patterns on pages 108-109)	3 large, 56 small
Leaves: (use pattern on page 109)	4 and 4R*
Top inner border: Cut crosswise	
Number of 2 1/2" strips	2
Top outer border: Cut crosswise	
Number of 5 1/2" strips	2
Bottom inner border: Cut crosswise	
Number of 4 1/2" strips	2
Bottom outer border: Cut crosswise	
Number of 7 1/2" strips	2
Backing: Piecing Diagram on page 103	A

*reverse template on fabric

CONSTRUCTION

1. Make two Square-in-a-Square blocks. Refer to the instructions on page 48 for help, if needed.

2. Cut the Square-in-a-Square blocks to make four Basket bottoms. Sew them together in a horizontal row and set aside.

3. Crease each 12 1/2" x 18 1/2" background block in half lengthwise to help with placement of stems. Sew the 12 1/2" x 18 1/2" background blocks together in a row. Appliquéing the shapes after the blocks are sewn together will allow for consistent placement.

4. To make the stems, fold the 2 1/4" x 16 1/2" strips in half lengthwise and press. Sew 1/8" from the edges to hold secure.

NOTE

Straight grain strips are used for the stems in this quilt because the stems are straight and do not require bias to curve.

5. Place the raw edge of each stem 1/4" to the left of each crease. Pin to hold in place. Then sew 1/4" from the raw edges. Press. Turn the fold over the stitching line, then either hand or machine stitch the folded edge to the background fabric.

6. Trace and cut plastic templates using the large leaf, small circle, and large circle patterns on page 108. Using your preferred method of appliqué, add them to the basket backgrounds. Refer to the instructions on page 98 for help, if needed.

7. Sew the appliquéd background row to the Basket row.

8. Piece the border strips as needed, then sew the inner and outer top borders together then attach to the top of the quilt. Repeat for the bottom border strips. Refer to instructions on page 102 for help, if needed.

FINISHING

Refer to the Backing Fabric and Batting instructions on page 103. Quilt as preferred, or see the instructions on page 104, if needed. Refer to the Binding instructions on page 106.

CHAPTER 6

House Block

House Block

12" block

This House block was designed to include a lawn or garden, window, and door, which can allow for a light source.

BLOCK SIZE: 12" finished
SHAPES: Squares and Rectangles
TECHNIQUES: Quick-cutting and strip-piecing
FABRIC SUGGESTIONS: Choose one fabric each for sky, chimneys, roof, house front, window, door, and ground.

How to make a House

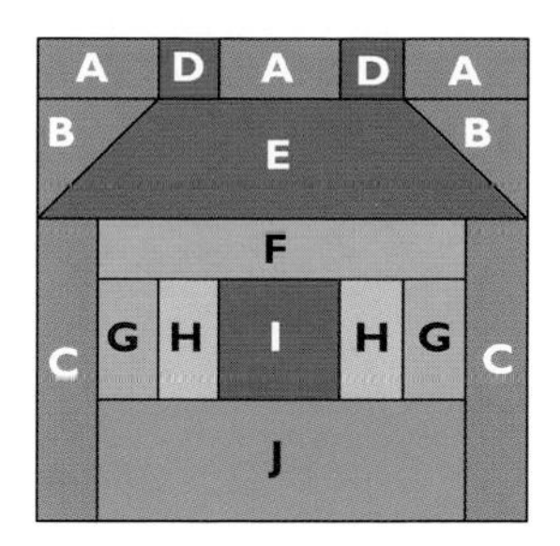

YARDAGE

To make one block:

$\frac{1}{8}$ yard **each** of seven fabrics

CUTTING

Sky:	(A): Cut three 2" x $3\frac{1}{2}$" pieces.
	(B): Cut two $3\frac{1}{2}$" squares.
	(C): Cut two 2" x 8" pieces.
Chimneys:	(D): Cut two 2" squares.
Roof:	(E): Cut one $3\frac{1}{2}$" x $12\frac{1}{2}$" piece.
House front:	(F): Cut one 2" x $9\frac{1}{2}$" piece.
	(G): Cut two 2" x $3\frac{1}{2}$" pieces.
Windows:	(H): Cut two 2" x $3\frac{1}{2}$" pieces.
Door:	(I): Cut one $3\frac{1}{2}$" square.
Ground:	(J): Cut one $3\frac{1}{2}$" x $9\frac{1}{2}$" piece.

CONSTRUCTION

1. Sew the sky (A) and chimney (D) pieces together, as shown. Press the seams toward the darker fabric.

Helpful Hint

When making several blocks, join $3\frac{1}{2}$" strips (sky) and 2" strips (chimney) together lengthwise. Cut every 2".

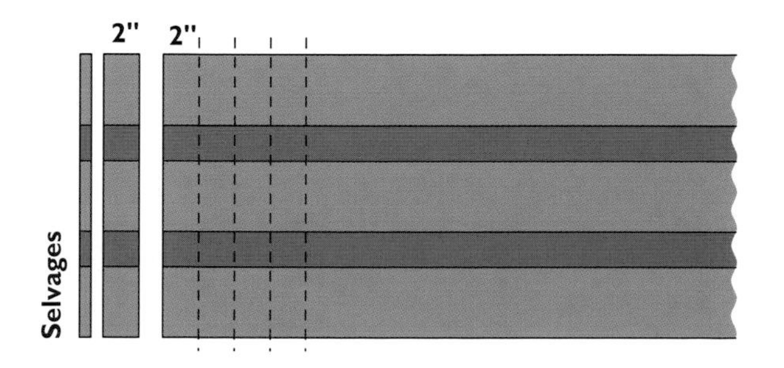

2. With right sides together, sew the sky (B) pieces and roof (E) piece together. Trim the back two layers to 1/4". Press the sky triangle over the stitching line. Repeat for the opposite side with the remaining sky piece.

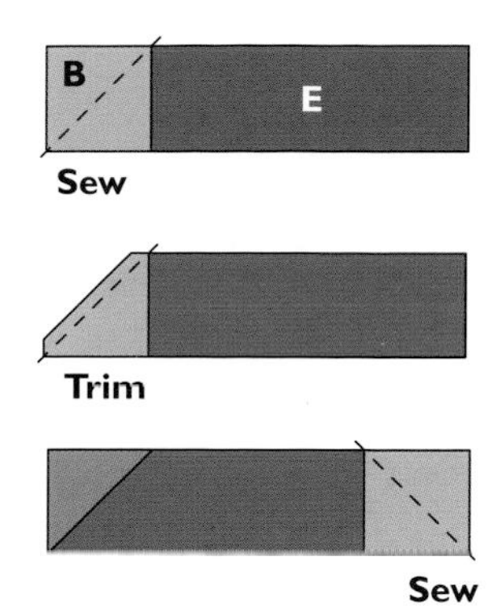

Helpful Hint

With right sides facing out, press the sky pieces in half diagonally. Use the crease as a sewing guide.

3. Sew the house front (G) and window (H) pieces together in pairs, then sew to the door (I).

G H I H G

Helpful Hint

When making several blocks, join 2" strips (house front and window) with $3\frac{1}{2}$" strip (door) lengthwise and then cut apart every $3\frac{1}{2}$".

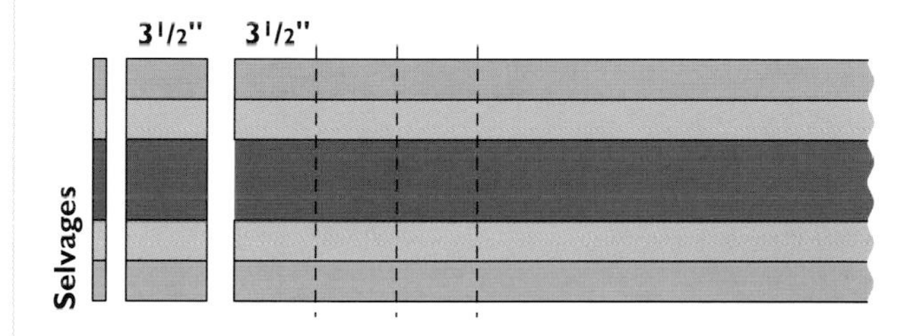

4. Sew the top house front (F) piece and ground (J) piece to the house/window/door unit. Press in the direction indicated by the arrows.

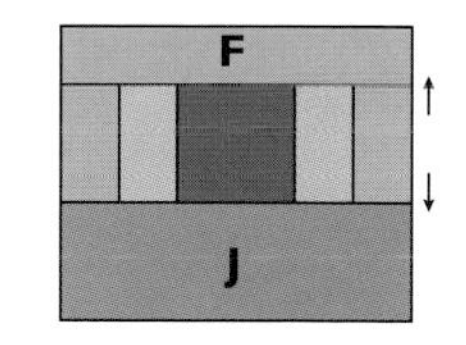

5. Attach the side sky (C) pieces, as shown. Press in the direction indicated by the arrows.

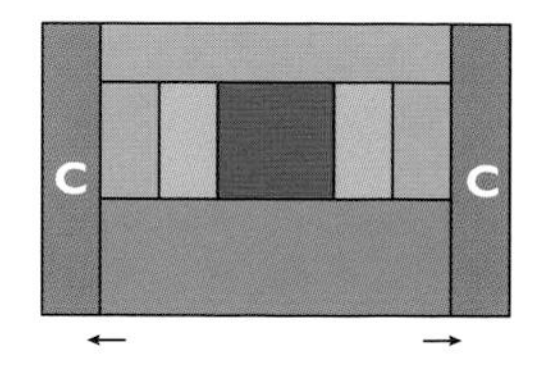

6. Sew all the units together to complete the block. Give the block a final press on the wrong, and then right side.

✔ Checkpoint

The block should measure $12\frac{1}{2}$" square.

The Big House

The Big House, 48" x 70½". Made by Diana McClun and Laura Nownes; machine quilted by Kathy Sandbach.

PATTERNS: House

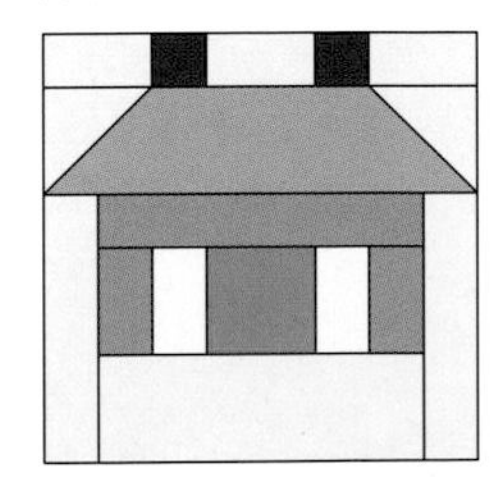

BLOCK SIZE: 12" finished

SETTING: Straight with sashing

TECHNIQUES: Quick-cutting and strip piecing

FABRIC AND COLOR INSPIRATION: White and neutral colors were used.

Finished size:	48" x 70$^1/_2$"
Blocks set	3 x 3
Number of blocks	9

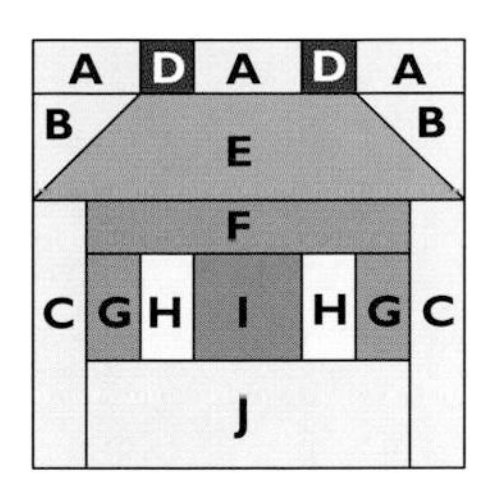

YARDAGE

Based on 42" fabric, from selvage to selvage

HOUSE BLOCKS:

Sky: fabrics to total	1
Chimneys: fabrics to total	1/4
Roofs: fabrics to total	1/2
House fronts: fabrics to total	1/2
Windows: fabrics to total	1/4
Doors: fabrics to total	3/8
Ground: fabrics to total	1/2
FENCE:	
Light fabric	3/8
Dark fabric (includes rail)	1/2
Sashing and border: Cut crosswise	1
Sky for large house	3/8
Roof for large house: Cut crosswise	3/4
or Cut lengthwise	1 1/2
Ground for large house: Cut crosswise	3/8
or Cut lengthwise	1 1/2
Backing	3
Binding (1/4" finished)	1/2

CUTTING

Use Quick-cutting techniques on page 95.

HOUSES:

Sky (A): Number of 2" x 3 1/2" pieces	27
(B): Number of 3 1/2" squares:	18
(C): Number of 2" x 8" rectangles:	18
Chimneys (D): Number of 2" squares	18
Roofs (E): Number of 3 1/2"x 12 1/2" pieces	9
House fronts (F): Number of 2" x 9 1/2" pieces	9
(G): Number of 2" x 3 1/2" pieces	18
Windows (H): Number of 2" x 3 1/2" pieces	18
Doors (I): Number of 3 1/2" squares	9
Ground (J): Number of 3 1/2" x 9 1/2" pieces	9
FENCE:	
Light fabric: Number of 1 1/2" strips	6
Dark fabric: Number of 1 1/2" strips	6
Number of 1" strips for railing	4
Sashing and borders: number of 3 1/2" strips	7
Cut two strips into 3 1/2" x 12 1/2"	
pieces for vertical sashing	6
(Use the remaining 5 strips for borders.)	
Sky (large house)**:** number of 12 1/2" squares	2
Large Roof: number of 12 1/2" strips	
Cut crosswise	1
or Cut lengthwise	2
Large Ground (bottom border): Number of 6 1/2" strips,	
Cut crosswise	2
or Cut lengthwise	1
Backing: Piecing Diagram page 103	B

CONSTRUCTION

1. Make nine House blocks. Refer to the instructions on page 63 for help, if needed.

2. Sew the blocks and vertical sashing strips together into horizontal rows.

3. Make the Fence including railing to the lengths needed. Refer to the instructions on page 17 for help, if needed.

4. Sew the Fence to the bottom of each horizontal row of blocks. Join the rows together.

5. Attach the borders to the top and bottom and then to the sides of the quilt top. Refer to page 102 for help, if needed.

6. Attach the large ground bottom border to the bottom of the quilt top.

7. Cut the length of the roof piece the same measurement as the width of the quilt top, seaming the large roof strips if necessary.

8. Place the large sky squares onto the roof piece, and sew diagonally across the squares of sky fabric, as shown. Trim the back two layers to 1/4" beyond the stitching line, as shown. Then press the sky triangle over the stitching line.

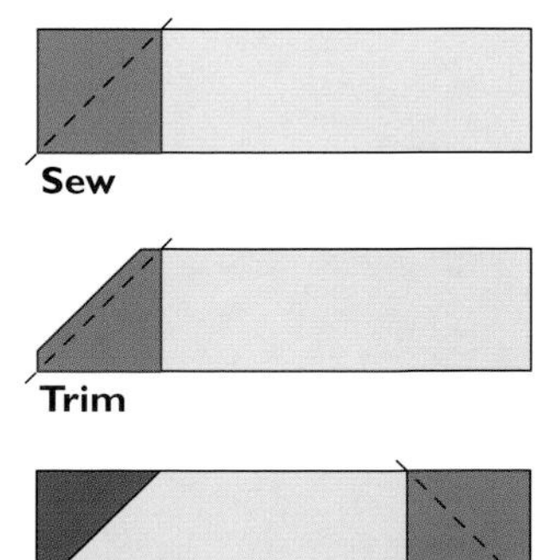

9. Sew the sky/roof border to the top edge of the quilt top.

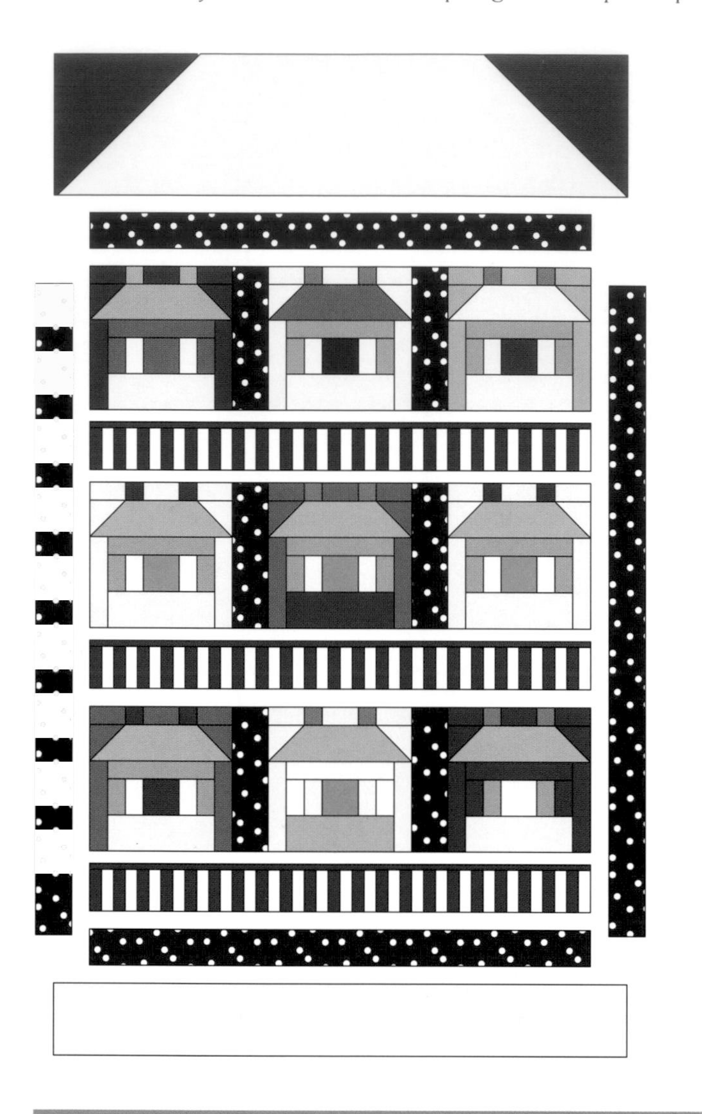

FINISHING

Refer to the Backing Fabric and Batting instructions on page 103. Quilt as preferred, or see instructions on page 104, if needed. Refer to the Binding instructions, page 106.

Topsey Turvey House

Topsey Turvey House, 64" x 64". Made by Diana McClun and Laura Nownes; machine quilted by Kathy Sandbach.

PATTERN: House and Crazy Patch

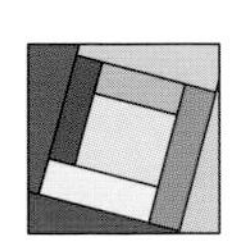

HOUSE BLOCK SIZE: 12" finished

TOPSEY TURVEY BLOCK SIZE: 16" finished

CRAZY PATCH BLOCK SIZE: 8" finished

SETTING: Straight

TECHNIQUES: Quick-cutting and strip piecing

FABRIC AND COLOR INSPIRATION: Collections of berries, fruits, and vegetable prints along with harvest scenes were used for the houses. Blue sky fabrics provide a background. Plaids and stripes in rich, warm tones were used to surround the House blocks. The crazy patch border uses all of the leftover fabrics.

	Photo Quilt	Queen	King
Finished size	64" x 64"	80" x 80"	96" x 96"
Blocks set	3 x 4	4 x 5	5 x 6
Number of House blocks	12	20	30
Number of Crazy Patch blocks	16	20	24

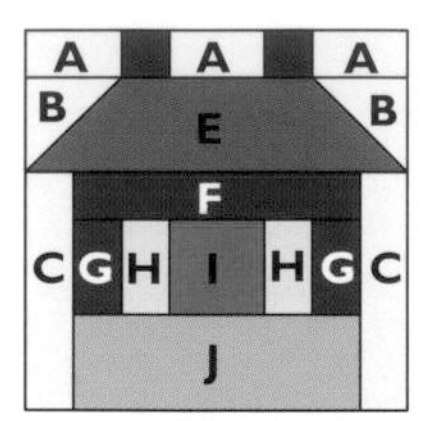

YARDAGE

Based on 42" wide fabric, from selvage to selvage

	Photo Quilt	Queen	King
HOUSE BLOCKS:			
Sky: fabrics to total	$1\frac{1}{2}$	$2\frac{1}{2}$	$3\frac{3}{4}$
or $\frac{1}{8}$ for **each** block			
Chimneys: fabrics to total	$\frac{1}{4}$	$\frac{1}{4}$	$\frac{1}{4}$
Roofs: fabrics to total	$\frac{3}{4}$	$1\frac{1}{8}$	$1\frac{3}{8}$
House fronts: fabrics to total	$\frac{3}{4}$	$1\frac{1}{8}$	$1\frac{3}{8}$
Windows: fabrics to total	$\frac{3}{8}$	$\frac{1}{2}$	$\frac{1}{2}$
Doors: fabrics to total	$\frac{3}{8}$	$\frac{3}{8}$	$\frac{1}{2}$
Ground: fabrics to total	$\frac{3}{8}$	$\frac{7}{8}$	$1\frac{1}{8}$
Strips around House blocks: fabrics to total			
(includes Crazy Patch strips)	$3\frac{1}{2}$	$5\frac{3}{4}$	$8\frac{1}{2}$
CRAZY PATCH BLOCKS:			
Crazy Patch Sky centers:	$\frac{1}{4}$	$\frac{1}{4}$	$\frac{3}{8}$
Foundation fabric:	$1\frac{1}{4}$	$1\frac{1}{2}$	$1\frac{3}{4}$
Backing	4	$7\frac{1}{4}$	$8\frac{5}{8}$
Binding ($\frac{1}{4}$" finished)	$\frac{1}{2}$	$\frac{5}{8}$	$\frac{5}{8}$

Helpful Hint

Save all of your fabric scraps as they will be used for the Crazy Patch blocks.

CUTTING

Use Quick-cutting techniques on page 95.

HOUSE BLOCKS:

Sky:	(A): Cut three 2" x $3\frac{1}{2}$" pieces.
	(B): Cut two $3\frac{1}{2}$" squares.
	(C): Cut two 2" x 8" pieces.
Chimneys:	(D): Cut two 2" squares.
Roof:	(E): Cut one $3\frac{1}{2}$" x $12\frac{1}{2}$" piece.
House front:	(F): Cut one 2" x $9\frac{1}{2}$" piece.
	(G): Cut two 2" x $3\frac{1}{2}$" pieces.
Windows:	(H): Cut two 2" x $3\frac{1}{2}$" pieces.
Door:	(I): Cut one $3\frac{1}{2}$" square.
Ground:	(J): Cut one $3\frac{1}{2}$" x $9\frac{1}{2}$" piece.

	Photo Quilt	Queen	King
Strips around House block:			
Number of 2" strips	24	40	60
Number of 3" strips	24	40	60
CRAZY PATCH BLOCKS:			
Foundation fabric:			
Number of 9" strips	4	5	6
Cut into 9" squares.	16	20	24
Crazy Patch center:			
Number of $3\frac{1}{2}$" strips	2	2	3
Cut into $3\frac{1}{2}$" squares	16	20	24
Backing: Piecing Diagram page 103	B	C	C

CONSTRUCTION

1. Make the required number of House blocks. Refer to instructions on page 63 for help, if needed.

2. To add the strips around the House blocks, it is important to add one 2" strip and one 3" strip to each side, but either size can be added first. Work counter-clockwise adding each new strip, as you would for a log cabin block. Trim the extra length of each strip even with the edge. Continue adding strips until the block measures $20\frac{1}{2}$" square.

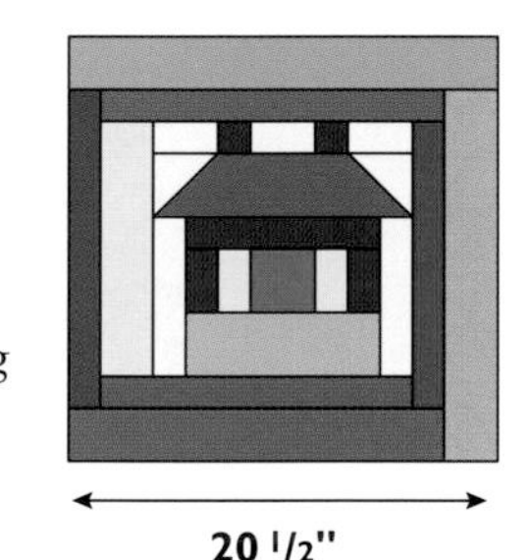

3. It is helpful to use a design wall to arrange the blocks to determine the placement.

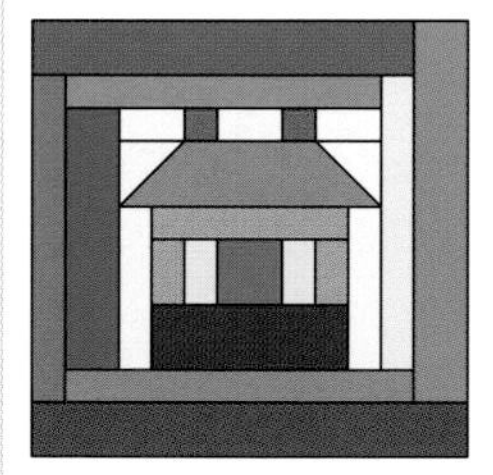
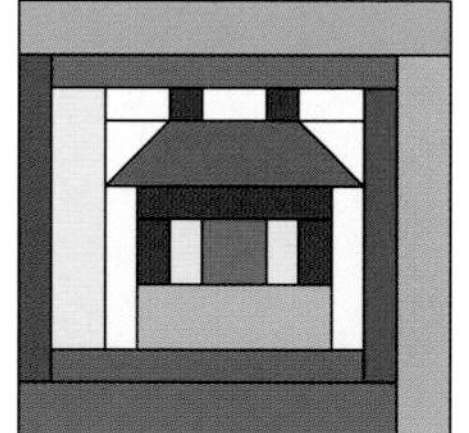
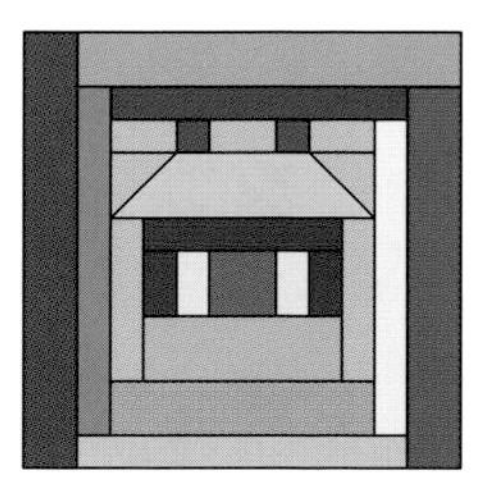

4. Label the House blocks by pinning a piece of paper to each block in order to identify its placement and whether the block will tilt to the left or right. Refer to the photo, page 67, to determine the tilt of each block.

Helpful Hint

Include this information on the paper labels: Row One—Block #1—Tilt left, Row One—Block #2—Tilt right, Row One—Block #3—Tilt left, etc.

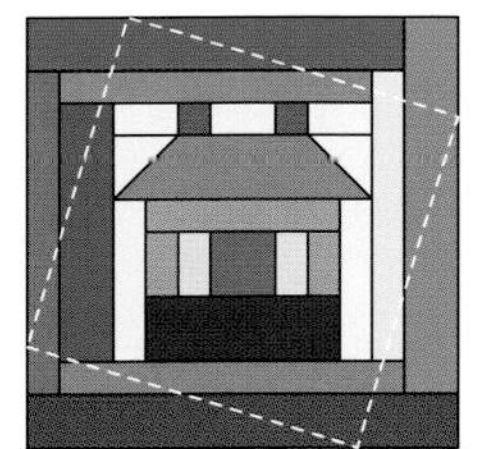

Row One
Block 1
Tilt left

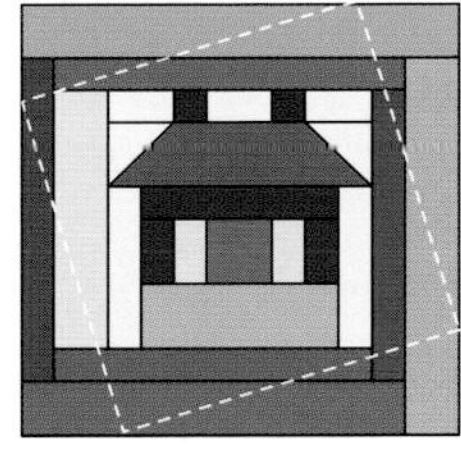

Row One
Block 2
Tilt right

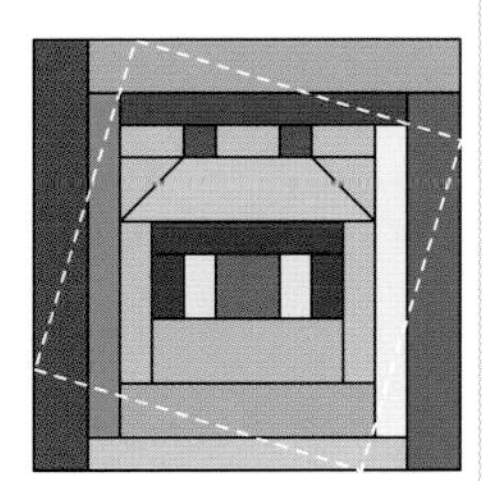

Row One
Block 3
Tilt left

5. You will need to trim each 20½" block at angles to make a 16 ½" block that has a tilt. Measure 4" in from each corner of the 20½" block. Mark and label these points A, B, C, and D. Connect points A and B with a ruler and trim using a rotary cutter. Continue around the block connecting B to C, C to D, and D to A, trimming the block as shown below. Save the trimmed corners to use in the Crazy Patch Blocks.

Note

To make a house that tilts to the right, measure 4" up from the bottom left corner of the 20½" block and continue around the block. To make a house that tilts to the left, measure 4" up from the bottom right corner of the 20½" block and continue around the block.

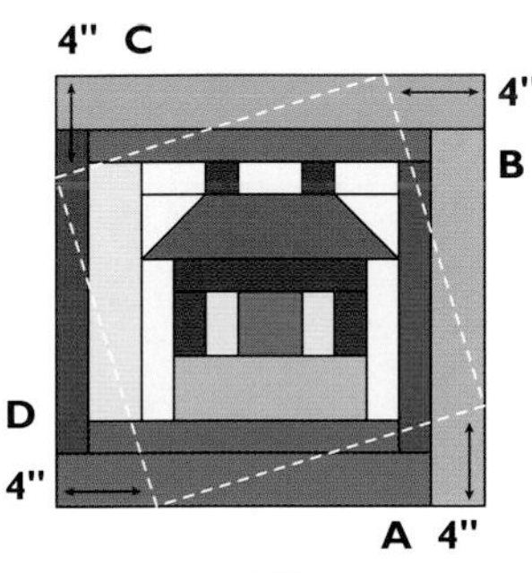

Right-hand Tilt

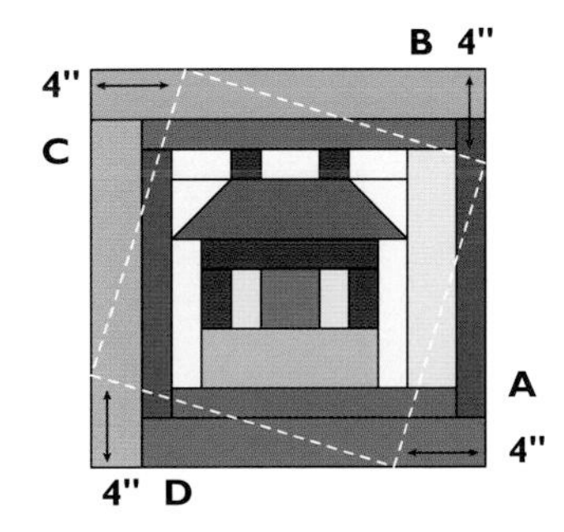

Left-hand Tilt

6. Arrange and sew the blocks together in a straight set. Press seams in one direction. Reverse the direction of the pressing for the next row.

Helpful Hint

Pin the blocks together carefully to prevent bias edges from stretching.

7. To make the Crazy Patch blocks: Place a square of sky fabric right side up at an angle close to the center of the foundation fabric.

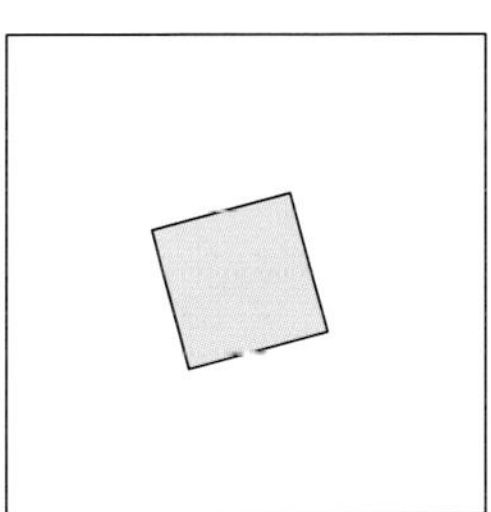

8. Choose a scrap of fabric that has a straight edge. Place it right side down onto the center square. Line up the straight edge with the edge of the center square. Stitch through all layers ¼" from the straight edge of the scrap.

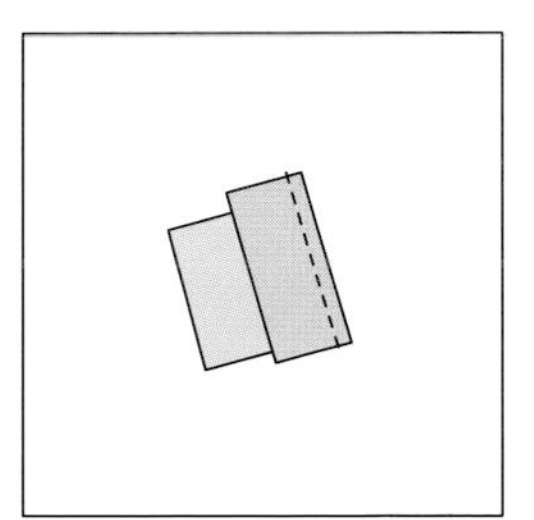

9. Fold the top scrap over the stitching line and finger press. Use scissors to trim the scrap even with the edge of the center square.

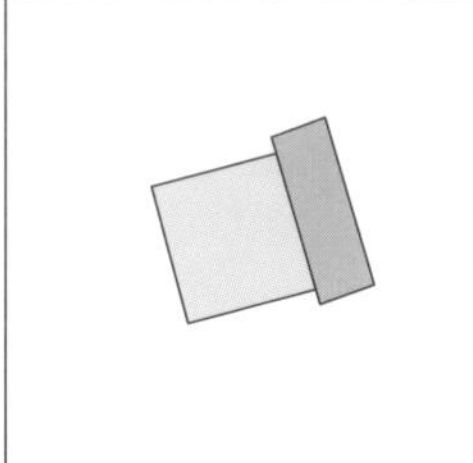

10. Rotate the block and then lay another scrap right side down, matching one of its sides to an unsewn side of the center square. Sew a 1/4" seam through all thickness.

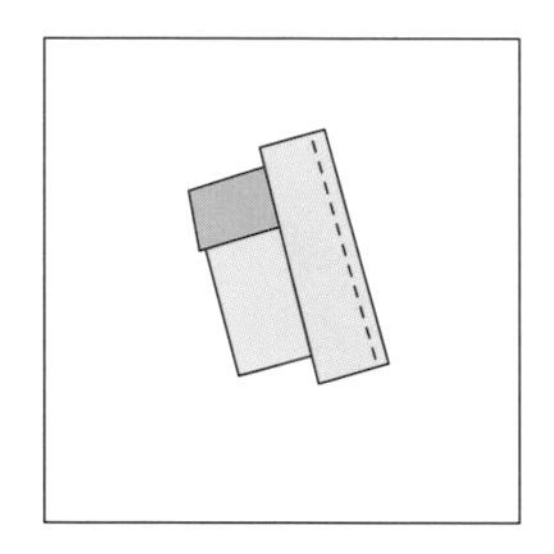

11. Fold this new shape back over the stitching line and finger press.

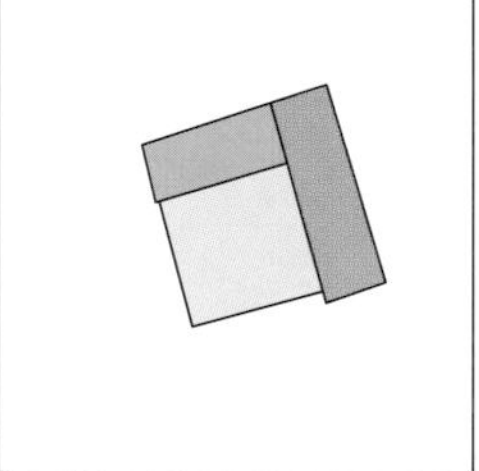

12. Continue working in the same manner around the center square until the foundation block is covered with fabric.

13. Use the cutting tools to straighten and trim the blocks to 8 1/2" square.

14. Arrange the Crazy Patch blocks in vertical rows to form the side borders. Sew blocks together and attach to the sides of the quilt top.

FINISHING

Refer to Backing Fabric and Batting instructions on page 103. Quilt as preferred, or see the instructions on page 104, if needed. Refer to the Binding instructions on page 106.

Sampler Quilts

CHAPTER 7

Harvest Time

Harvest Time, 44" x 44". Made by Diana McClun and Laura Nownes; machine quilted by Kathy Sandbach.

PATTERNS: Nine-Patch, Fence, Square-in-a-Square Basket variation, Half-Square triangles, Tree, and House

TECHNIQUES: Quick-cutting, strip piecing, half-square triangles, quarter-square triangles

FABRIC AND COLOR INSPIRATION: The lush fruit fabric used on the top and bottom border was the inspiration for the harvest theme. Other fabrics were chosen to continue the theme.

TO MAKE THIS QUILT

Nine-Patch blocks, page 15	6
Basket blocks, page 51,	3
Half-Square triangles, page 27	22
Fence, page 17	84"
Tree blocks, page 44	2
House block, page 63	1

YARDAGE

Based on 42" wide fabric, from selvage to selvage

Nine-Patch blocks: 1/4 yard **each** of three fabrics

Basket blocks: 1/8 yard **each** of three fabrics

Basket bases and backgrounds: 1/4 yard each of **two** fabrics

Half-Square triangles: Use leftover pieces from other blocks or 1/2 yard **each** of light fabrics and dark fabrics.

Fence: 3/8 yard of light fabric, 3/8 yard of dark fabric and 1/8 yard of fabric for the railing.

Trees: 1/4 yard **each** of two fabrics (sky and tree(, 1/8 yard for trunks

House: 1/8 yard **each** of seven fabrics

Large print border: 1/2 yard

Backing: 2 3/4 yards

Binding: (1/4" finished) 3/8 yard

CUTTING

Top large print strip (above baskets): Cut one 6 1/2" x 36 1/2" piece.

Lower large print strip (below fence): Cut one 7 1/2" x 36 1/2" piece.

Sky pieces (above short Fence strips): Cut two 6 1/2" x 9" rectangles.

Fence: Cut six 1 1/2" strips of light. Cut six 1 1/2" strips of dark. Cut four 1" strips for railing.

Backing: Piecing Diagram A, page 103

Winter Fun

Winter Fun, 48" x 56". Made by Diana McClun and Laura Nownes; machine quilted by Kathy Sandbach.

PATTERNS: Nine-Patch, Fence, Square-in-a-Square, Half-Square triangle, Birdhouse, and House

TECHNIQUES: Quick-cutting, strip piecing, half-square triangles, quarter-square triangles, and appliqué

FABRIC AND COLOR INSPIRATION: The inspiration for *Winter Fun* came from fabrics that represented snow, snowmen, and the cold weather holidays. Using these fabrics as a guide, greens, reds, pure white, and blues were added, using a variety of prints. Once the theme was established, the coordinating fabrics were chosen which represent snow on the roof, nighttime sky, birdhouses, etc.

TO MAKE THIS QUILT

Nine-Patch blocks, page 15	6
Fence: (with 1" railing), page 17	48"
Square-in-a-Square blocks, page 48	4
Half-Square triangles, page 27	44
Birdhouse blocks, page 44	4
House blocks, page 63	4

YARDAGE

Based on 42" wide fabric, from selvage to selvage

Nine-Patch blocks: 1/4 yard **each** of three fabrics

Fence: 1/4 yard **each** of two fabrics

Square-in-a-Square blocks: 1/4 yard of **each** four fabrics

Half-Square triangles and corner squares: 5/8 yard **each** of two fabrics

Birdhouse blocks: 1/4 yard **each** of three fabrics (sky, roof, and house) and 1/8 yard **each** of two fabrics (circle and pole)

House blocks: 1/4 yard **each** of seven to ten fabrics

Red strips below fence: 1/8 yard

Inner side borders: 1/4 yard

Backing: 3 yards

Binding: (1/4" finished) 1/2 yard

CUTTING

Fence: Cut three 1 1/2" strips of light. Cut three 1 1/2" strips of dark. Cut two 1" strips for railing.

Red strips below fence: Cut four 1 1/2" x 12 1/2" pieces.

Side inner borders: Cut three 2 1/2" strips.

Border corners: Cut four 4 1/2" squares.

Backing: Piecing Diagram A, page 103

CONSTRUCTION

The Birdhouse blocks need to measure 6 1/2" x 17". Trim any excess from the top to obtain this measurement.

Celebration of Summer

Celebration of Summer, 43" x 51". Made by Diana McClun and Laura Nownes; machine quilted by Kathy Sandbach.

PATTERNS: Nine-Patch, Fence, Square-in-a-Square Basket variation, Half-Square triangle, House, and Appliqué

TECHNIQUES: Quick-cutting, strip piecing, half-square triangles, quarter-square triangles, and appliqué

FABRIC AND COLOR INSPIRATION: The red batik used in the background was the inspiration and provided us with the direction for the colors used throughout the quilt.

TO MAKE THIS QUILT

Nine-Patch blocks, page 15 (two combinations of three fabrics **each**)	16
Fence: (without railing), page 17	91"
Square-in-a-Square block, pages 48 and 51 Cut in half diagonally. You will use one.	1
Half-Square triangles, page 27	12
House blocks, page 63	3
Stems	3
Large Leaves: pattern page 109	1 and 1R*
Small Circles: pattern page 108	10
Large Circles: pattern page 109	2
Flowers: pattern page 109	3 and 3R*
Birds: pattern page 108	1 and 1R*
Butterflies: pattern page 108	2

*R= reverse pattern on fabric

YARDAGE

Based on 42" wide fabric, from selvage to selvage

Nine-Patch blocks: 1/4 yard **each** of six fabrics

Fence: 3/8 yard **each** of two fabrics

Half-Square triangles: 1/4 yard **each** of two fabrics

Houses: 1/8 yard **each** of seven fabrics for **each** House

Background: 3/4 yard

Square-in-a-Square for Basket: 1/8 yard **each** of three fabrics

Basket base: 1/4 yard

Stems: one 18" x 22" piece (fat quarter)

Leaves: 1/8 yard

Circles: 1/8 yard total

Flowers: 1/8 yard total

Birds: 1/8 yard

Butterflies: 1/4 yard total

Backing: 2 3/4 yards

Binding: (1/4" finished) 3/8 yard

CUTTING

Red basket background:

Cut one 24 1/2" x 24 1/2" piece (top).

Cut two 6 1/2" squares (bottom sides).

Fence: cut six 1 1/2" strips **each** of two fabrics.

Leaves and Birds: Cut one and one reversed **each**.

Stems: Cut three 2" bias strips, **each** at least 20" long.

Backing: Piecing Diagram B, page 103

Rebirth of the Garden

Rebirth of the Garden, 52" x 75". Made by Diana McClun and Laura Nownes; machine quilted by Kathy Sandbach.

PATTERNS: Nine-Patch, Fence, Square-in-a-Square, Half-Square triangle, Birdhouse, Quarter-Square triangle, House, and Appliqué.

TECHNIQUES: Quick cutting, strip piecing, half-square triangles, quarter-square triangles, and appliqué

FABRIC AND COLOR INSPIRATION: The inspiration for this quilt came from the fabric line "Color Profusion", by Susie Robbins for P&B Textiles. The addition of solids and tone-on-tones give the eyes a resting place from the bright and intense fabrics and help showcase the collection.

TO MAKE THIS QUILT

House blocks, page 63	6
Nine-Patch blocks, page 15 (two combinations of three fabrics **each**)	6
Fence with 1" rail, page 17	176"
Square-in-a-Square blocks, page 48	4
Half-Square triangles, page 27	31
Birdhouse blocks, page 44	5
Small circles, pattern page 108 5 for Birdhouses and 5 for Butterfly strip	10
Large circles, pattern page 109 for Square-in-a-Square strip	10
Birds, pattern page 108	1 and 2R*
Butterflies, pattern page 108	4

*R= reverse pattern on fabric

YARDAGE

Based on 42" wide fabric, from selvage to selvage

Nine-Patch blocks: 1/4 yard **each** of six fabrics

Fence: 1/2 yard dark and 5/8 yard light (includes railing)

Half-Square triangles: Use leftovers from sky and house plus 3 to 4 additional fabrics to total 3/8 yard light **and** 3/8 dark.

Square-in-a-Square: 3/8 yard **each** of two fabrics for strips, for center use scraps from house windows, 1 yard for setting triangles

Birdhouses: 1 yard for sky, 1/8 yard for poles, 1/4 yard for house. Roof fabrics are scraps to total 1/4 yard from House blocks

House: 3/8 **each** of two fabrics for sky, 1/4 yard **each** of six other fabrics

Birds, Butterflies, and Circles: Scraps from window and house fabrics

Butterfly background: 1/4 yard

Backing: 3 1/4 yards

Binding: (1/4" finished) 1/2 yard

CUTTING

Fence: Light: Cut nine 1 1/2" strips and five 1" strips (railing). Dark: Cut nine 1 1/2" strips.

Two sky pieces on sides of Birdhouse blocks: Cut two pieces 11 1/2" x 15 1/2".

Background for the Butterfly strip: Cut one piece 7 1/2" x 36 1/2".

Birdhouse blocks: For this quilt three of the bottom pole units are cut 6 1/2" x 4 1/2. The two remaining pole units are cut 6 1/2" x 6 1/2". After completing the blocks, the upper sky fabric is trimmed so all the Birdhouse blocks measure 6 1/2" x 15 1/2".

Setting triangles for the Square-in-a-Square strip: Cut two 15" squares for the top and bottom triangles. Cut the squares into **quarters** diagonally to make triangles.

Corner triangles: Cut two 12" squares. Cut the squares in **half** diagonally to make triangles.

Backing: Piecing Diagram B, page 103

CONSTRUCTION

The setting triangles will be a little larger than needed. Trim the Square-in-a-Square strip 1/2" beyond the corners of the blocks on the top and bottom. Trim the length as needed when joining it to the top section of the quilt top.

CHAPTER 8

Gallery

Home for the Season, $27^{1}/_{2}$" x 29".
Made by Lyn Kelly;
machine quilted by Kathy Sandbach.

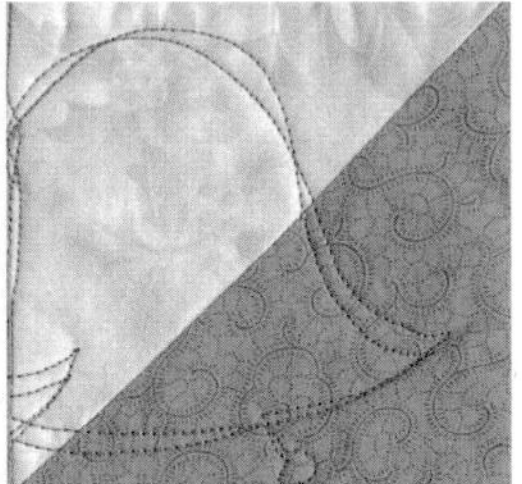

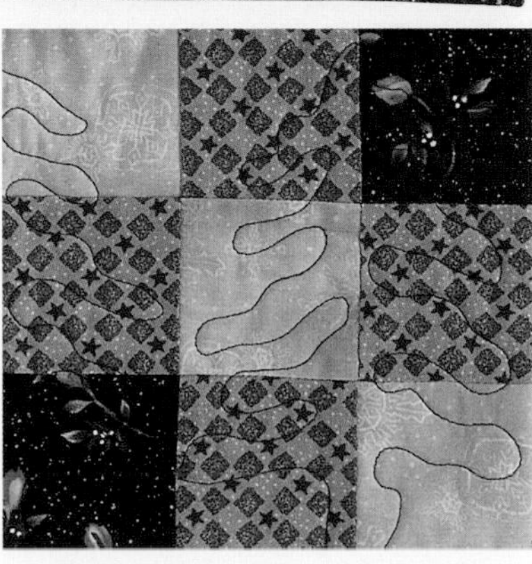

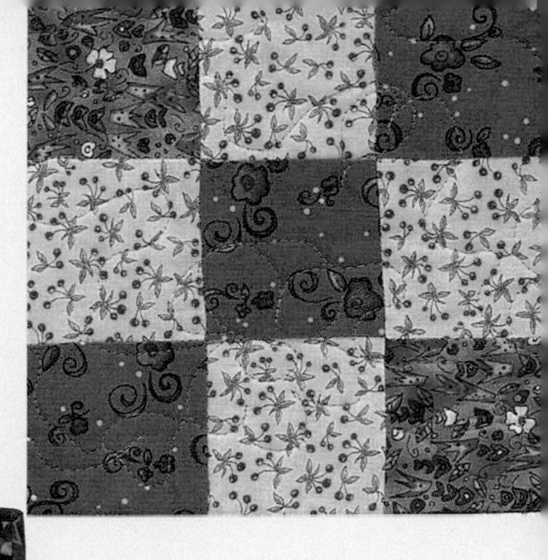

A Quilt for Diana, 45" x 39½". Made by Carolyn Brien; machine quilted by Kathy Sandbach.

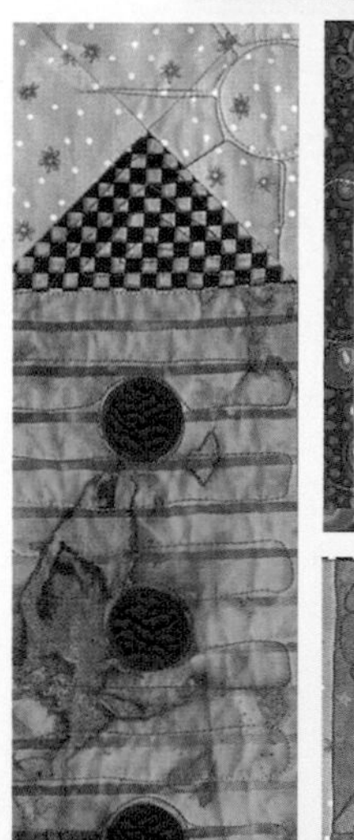

Home Tweet Home, 65" x 75".
Made by Liberty Palfreyman;
machine quilted by Kathy Sandbach.

Simply Folk Art, 59" x 62".
Made by Kathy Kluba August;
machine quilted by Lynne Todoroff.

Dillon Beach, 40" x 47".
Made by Debbie Hofmeister;
machine quilted by Kathy Sandbach.

Summer in the Neighborhood, 55" x 55".
Made and quilted by Laurie Rabinowitz.

Serendipity, 46" x 51".
Made by Sue Wakefield; machine quilted by Lynne Todoroff.

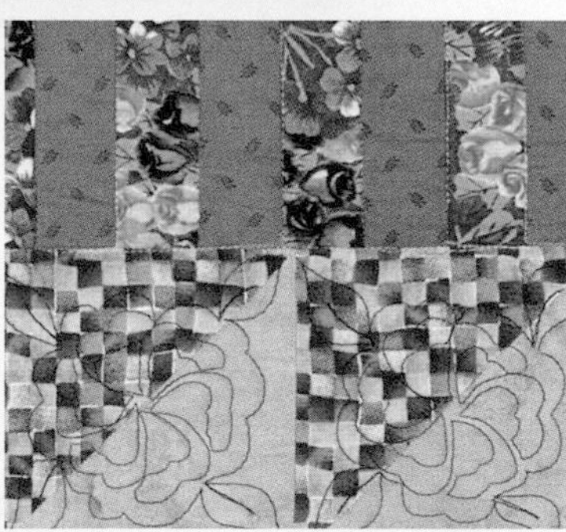

Little Dutch Town, 56" x 74".
Made by Sandra Marie Jorgenson;
machine quilted by Lynne Todoroff.

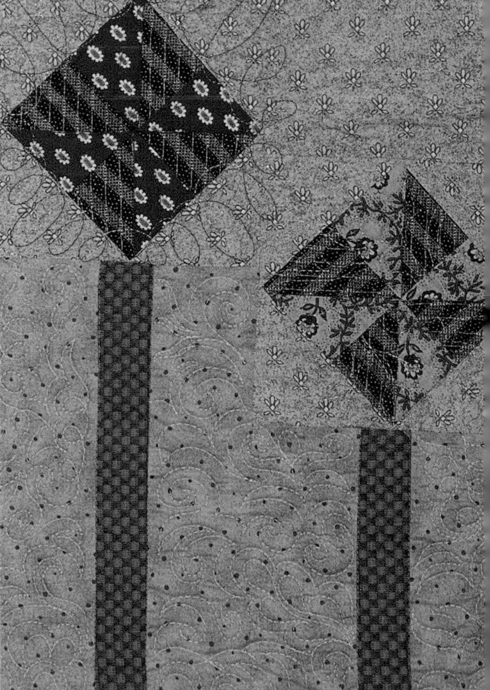

Oma's Garden, 70½" x 70".
Made by Ria Wallmann;
machine quilted by Kathy Sandbach.

Tropical Houses, 56" x 48".
Made by Diana McClun and Laura Nownes; machine quilted by Kathy Sandbach.

The Funny Farm, 56" x 58".
Made by Jean Crisp;
machine quilted by Kathy Sandbach.

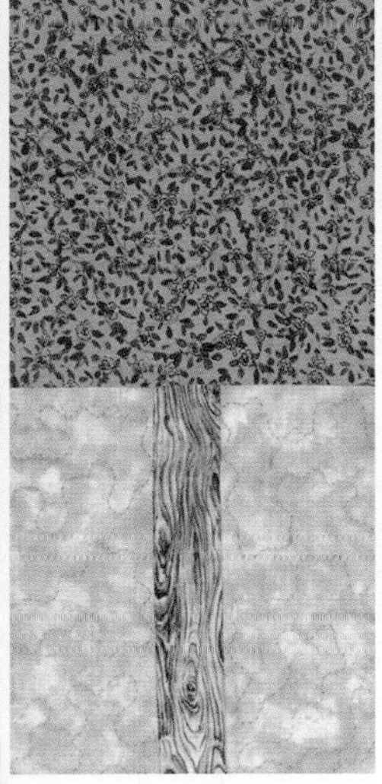

My English Garden, 51" x 43".
Made by Robin J. Olvera;
machine quilted by Anna White.

Night and Day, 59" x 79".
Made and quilted by Nancy Donahoe.

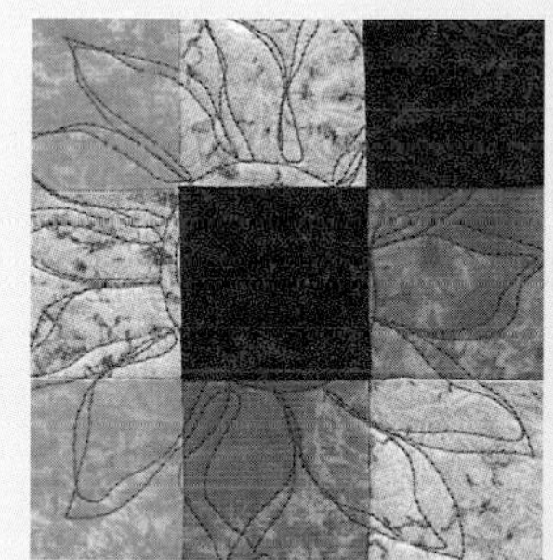

The Garden Houses,
44" x 46½".
Made by Kathy Kluba August;
machine quilted by Kathy Sandbach.

CHAPTER 9

General Instructions and Techniques

Prepare the Fabric for Cutting

To prewash or not to prewash, that is the question

You have three choices before cutting into your fabric:

1. Prewash and preshrink: The fabric can be pre-washed and pre-shrunk before cutting. First, unfold and wash the lights and darks separately in a washing machine with warm water and laundry soap. Tumble dry until slightly damp, then press.

2. Preshrink: This process will only preshrink the fabric, not remove all of the chemicals. Place the unfolded fabric in a sink full of warm water. Rinse thoroughly. Tumble dry until slightly damp, then press.

3. Work with "new" fabric: Use the fabric as it comes off the bolt. There is always a risk that a fabric will release excess dye and bleed into another lighter fabric when washed. There are products available, such as Retayne™, which can be used to prevent this from occurring when you wash the quilt for the first time.

Pressing and Straightening Fabric

Press the fabric to eliminate the crease that was created when it was rolled on the bolt. Fold the fabric in half lengthwise, right sides out, with the selvage edges together, while holding it in front of you. The selvage edges should be as even as possible (since selvages are tightly woven, sometimes the edges ripple. Just do your best). Look at the fold on the bottom. It should be smooth and without ripples. If it does ripple, slide one selvage edge to the right or left until the folded edge is smooth. In doing this, the cut edges (crosswise grain) may not match. This edge will be straightened with the first cut. The fabric is now accurately folded and ready to cut.

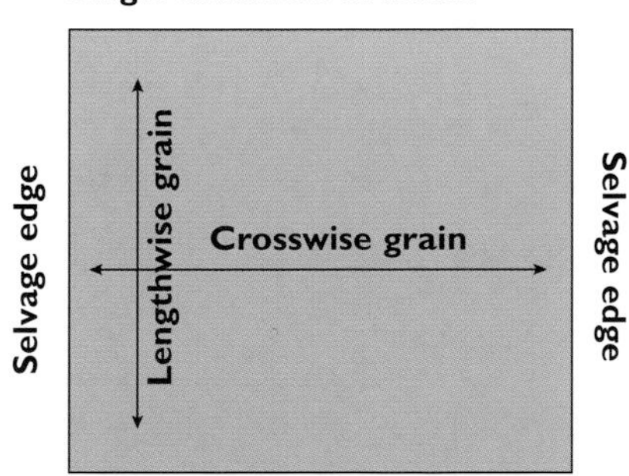

Cut edges may not be even when fabric is folded.

Quick-Cutting Fabric

Quick-cutting fabric using a rotary cutter, cutting mat and wide plastic ruler is an accurate and time-saving technique. The fabric is first cut into strips and then can be cut into other shapes such as squares, rectangles or triangles.

Use a level work surface that is a comfortable height for you. Bending over for long periods of time can cause back discomfort.

1. Place the accurately folded fabric onto the cutting mat, aligning the selvages with a horizontal line on the mat. Bring the fold even with the selvages. There are now four thickness. When cutting fat quarters, which are 18" x 22" pieces, leave them folded at double thickness, otherwise the piece becomes too narrow.

HELPFUL HINT

If you are working with a directional fabric, such as a stripe or plaid, it is best to cut through only one thickness at a time (on the lengthwise grain) in order to cut accurately along the printed lines or patterns.

NOTE

The following instructions are for right-handed people, left-handed people should reverse the placement.

2. To make the first cut and straighten the edges, place the ruler in line with a vertical line on the board, covering just the edges of all thicknesses on the left-hand side. With the fingers of your left hand in the upright position, press firmly on the ruler to hold it securely on the fabric. Hold the rotary cutter with your right hand by placing the handle in the palm of your hand and extending your index finger onto the outer circular part of the cutter. This will give a more accurate cut and prevent the cutter from swerving away from the ruler while cutting. Run the rotary cutter along the right-hand edge of the ruler, cutting through all thicknesses. Keep the blade tight against the ruler. Lift the ruler and remove the excess only, keeping the fabric accurately positioned on the board.

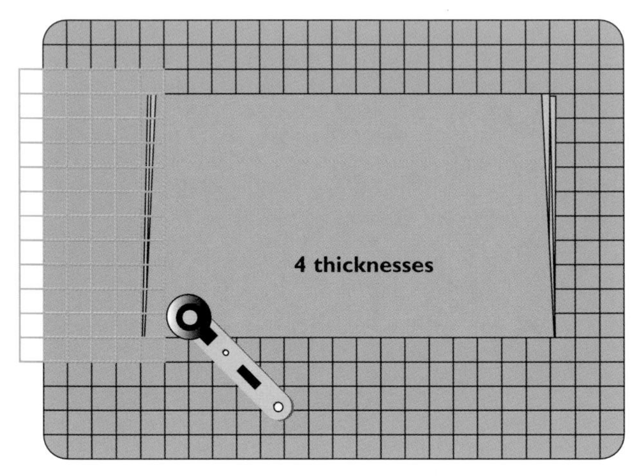

3. To cut strips, determine the width of the strip to be cut as indicated in each project. Align that marking on the ruler even with the newly cut edges of the fabric. Use the rotary cutter to accurately cut a strip of fabric the needed width.

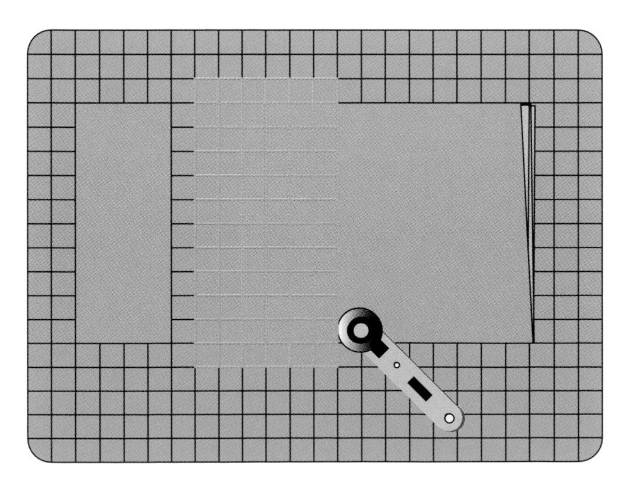

Helpful Hint

Accuracy and consistency is important every step of the way. Small variations in cutting can prevent your blocks from finishing to the correct size. Check the width of your first strip before cutting additional strips of the same size. Also, unfold the strip to see that it is without a bend where the fabric was folded. If a bend occurs, repress and refold the fabric, and straighten the edge before cutting additional strips.

4. To cut squares or rectangles from strips, place an accurately cut strip of fabric onto the cutting mat, using the marked lines on the mat for placement, as shown. Use the ruler and rotary cutter to cut the desired size squares or rectangles.

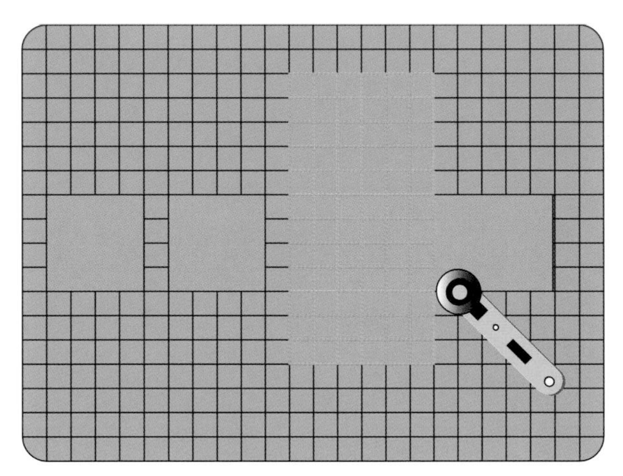

Cutting squares from strips

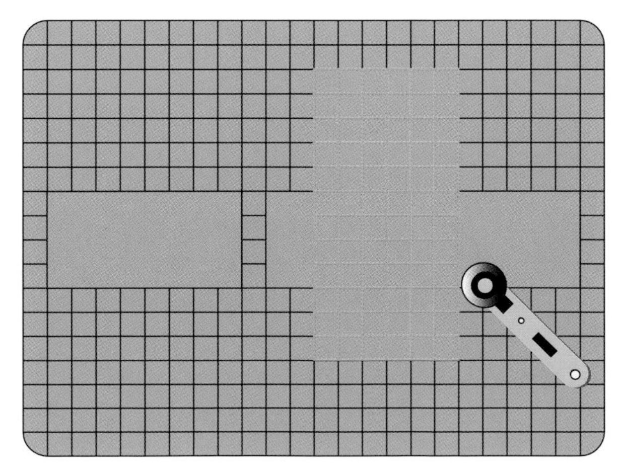

Cutting rectangles from strips

5. To cut half-square and quarter-square triangles, place accurately cut squares (no more than four layers) onto the cutting mat, using the marked lines on the mat for placement. To make an accurate diagonal cut, position the rotary cutter blade, firmly into the bottom corners of the squares. Bringing the ruler up tight against the blade, position the ruler corner to corner and cut the square in half diagonally.

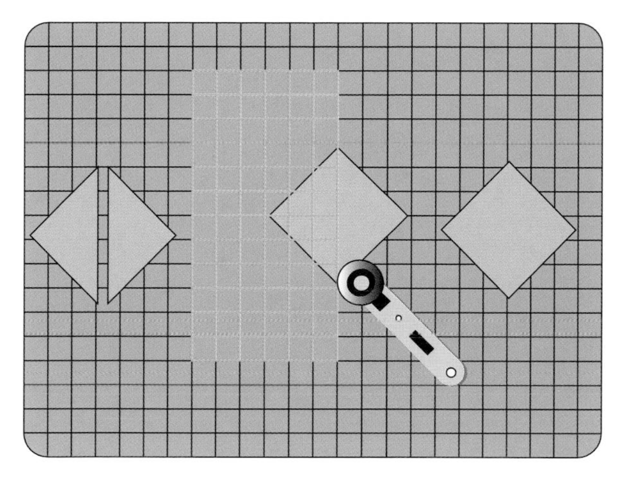

Cutting half-square triangles from squares

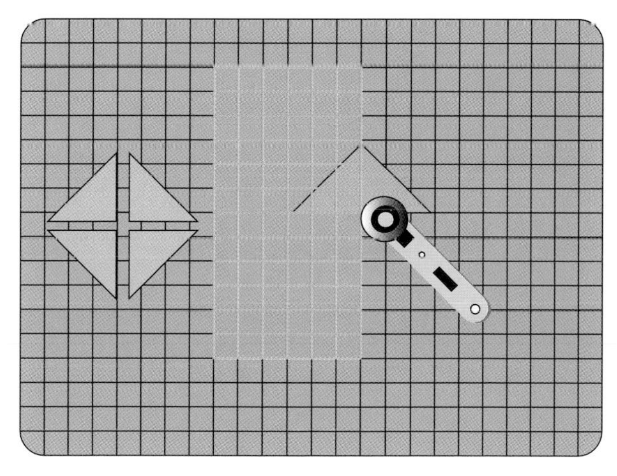

Cutting quarter-square triangles from squares

Preparation for Sewing

Establish an accurate 1/4" seam allowance

A 1/4" seam allowance is used in most quiltmaking. The seam allowance is the distance from the cut edge of the fabric to the line of stitching.

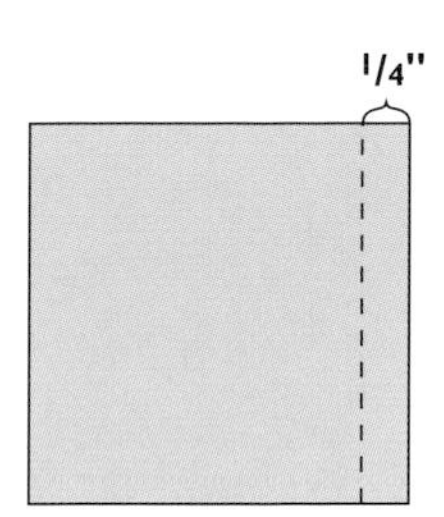

1/4" from cut edge to stitching line

An accurate 1/4" seam allowance is important to the success of your quilt blocks.

Helpful Hint

If you are hand piecing, use a marking pencil to indicate the stitching line on the wrong side of the fabric shapes.

If you are using a machine, check to see if the distance from the needle to the right-hand edge of the presser foot measures 1/4". If not, see if there is a needle position option on your machine, which will allow using the right-hand edge of the presser foot as a guide. If neither of these are options for you, consider making a "wall of masking tape" (approximately 6 layers thick) which is secured at the exact right position onto the throat plate of the sewing machine. The tape will help keep the fabric straight while sewing, and prevent the pieces from going beyond the 1/4".

Checkpoint:

Make a practice piece before sewing your project quilt. Cut three 1 1/2" x 3 1/2" pieces of fabric. Sew them together. Press the seams to one direction. (Refer to Pressing on page 98) Does the piece measure 3 1/2" x 3 1/2"? Is the center strip exactly 1" from seam to seam? If so, then you can feel secure about starting on your project quilt. If not, make the necessary adjustments, either cutting, seam allowance or pressing.

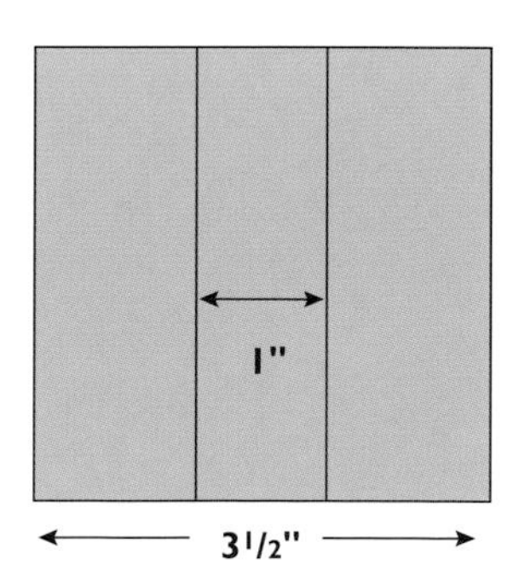

Sewing Machine: Is it Running Smoothly?

If using a sewing machine, check to see that it is running smoothly. Use 100% cotton sewing thread (not the heavier quilting thread) in a neutral color for both the top and bobbin. Use a 80/12 Universal needle. Clean the bobbin area to remove any threads and lint.

Sewing (Piecing)

Fabric pieces can be sewn together either with hand or machine stitches.

1. Place pieces right sides together. Stitch them together with a 1/4" seam allowance. Make sure that the raw edges are aligned with each other.

Note

If piecing by hand, use a quilting needle (called Betweens, number 8 or 9) and quilting thread in a neutral color. Join the pieces together with small running stitches 1/4" from the edges. Begin and end the line of stitching with two small back stitches.

2. Additional units can be stitched by continuing the chain of thread (chaining).

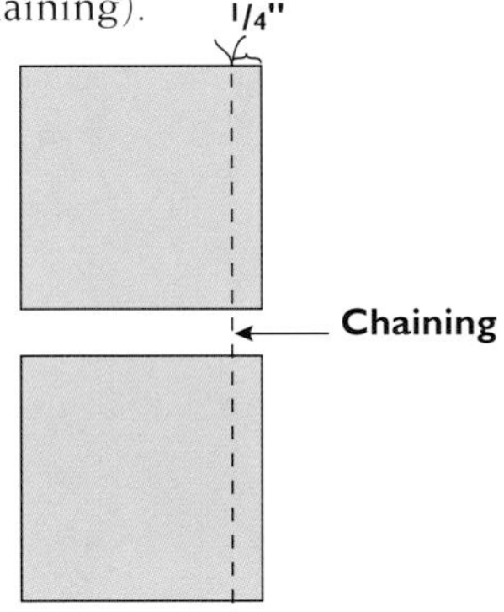

3. Cut the chain of thread, then press the new units.

Strip Piecing

Fabric strips can be sewn together on the sewing machine in desired combinations. The sewn strips can be cut apart to make new units. The width of the cut strips and the distance between the cuts is determined by the individual project.

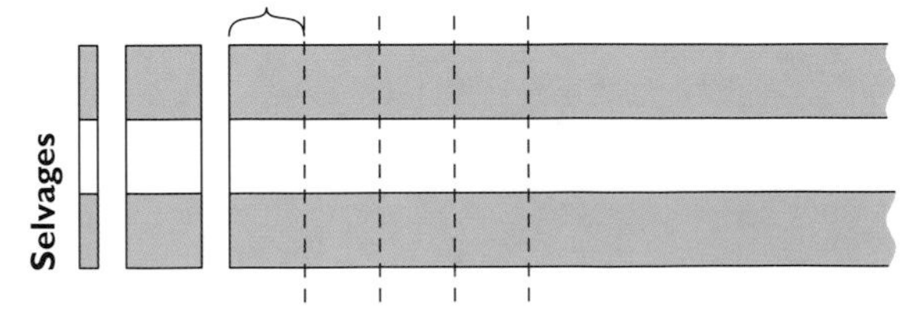

Pressing

Pressing is a very important part of quiltmaking. Get into the habit of pressing often. We make a distinction between pressing and ironing. Pressing is an up and down motion that will not distort the pieces or block. Set your iron on the cotton setting. Add water for steam. Use a firm pressing surface, which has been covered with a light-colored towel or piece of flannel.

Press the seam allowance flat on the wrong side first to flatten and set the machine stitches, then press on the right side. Whenever possible, press the seam allowance in the direction of the darker fabric to avoid a dark shadow under the lighter fabric.

Allow the fabric to cool before removing it from the pressing surface to avoid possible distortion. Use spray sizing or starch on the finished blocks, if desired.

Helpful Hint

Avoid overhandling the blocks because they are fragile and can stretch along the edges.

Appliqué

Appliqué is a technique used to attach a shape (such as a circle or leaf) to a background fabric. Here are two ways to prepare your shapes for appliqué that work well on the shapes included in this book. Once the shapes are prepared, you can sew them onto the background fabric either by hand or machine.

Method One: Paper Basting with Freezer Paper

Use plastic-coated freezer paper, which can be purchased in your local grocery store.

1. Use a pencil to trace the shape onto the paper side—not the shiny, plastic side—of the freezer paper.

2. Use paper scissors to cut the shape on the drawn line.

3. Use a dry iron to press the shiny side of the freezer paper shape onto the wrong side of the fabric.

4. Use fabric scissors to cut the fabric 1/4" beyond the edge of the paper.

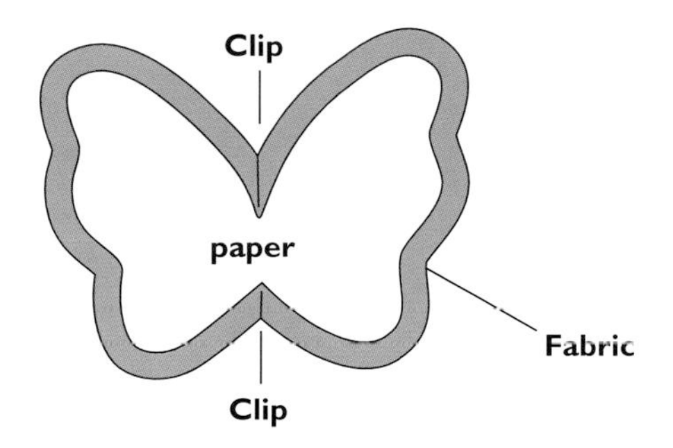

Cut fabric 1/4" beyond paper.

5. Using the edge of the paper as a guide, carefully turn the 1/4" extension to the wrong side of the shape and hand baste (temporary small running stitches) around the edges, through all layers. Press the shape first on the wrong and then right side.

6. Position the shape onto the background fabric and secure with basting stitches, or pins.

7. Use a small hand stitch or a machine blanket stitch to sew the edges of the shape to the background.

8. After the shape has been stitched to the background fabric, remove the basting stitches and then carefully cut out the background fabric from the back of the shape, to within 1/4" of the stitching line. Peel off and remove the paper pattern.

Method Two: Fusible or Transfer Web

Use a product such as TransWeb™ or Wonder Under™ which can be purchased at your local quilt or fabric store.

1. Trace the shape onto the paper side of the bonding material. Remember to trace the image **reversed** from how you want it to appear on the quilt. Use paper scissors to cut out the shapes, leaving at least 1/2" outside the drawn lines.

2. Follow the manufacturer's instructions for bonding the fusible material to the wrong side of your fabric. Cut out the shapes on the drawn lines.

3. Follow the manufacturer's instructions for removing the paper backing. Then fuse the fabric shape onto the background fabric.

Optional: Use a decorative stitch such as a hand or machine blanket stitch around the edges of the shape.

Helpful Hint

Making a permanent template out of plastic template material can be useful when you need multiple numbers of a shape. Use the template to trace onto freezer paper or paper-backed fusible web.

Hand Appliqué

If you do not want your stitches to show, use a small invisible stitch (called a Back Whip stitch) to secure the shape to the background fabric. Make small stitches into the background fabric then insert the needle into the folded edge of the shape. This stitch will hold the shape securely on the background.

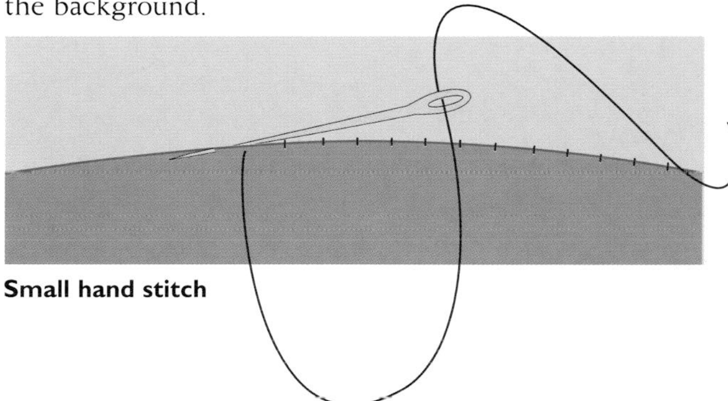

Small hand stitch

Hand Blanket stitches make an attractive edge on an appliquéd shape. Use an embroidery needle and two strands of embroidery floss or one strand of perle cotton to make stitches around the edge of the shape.

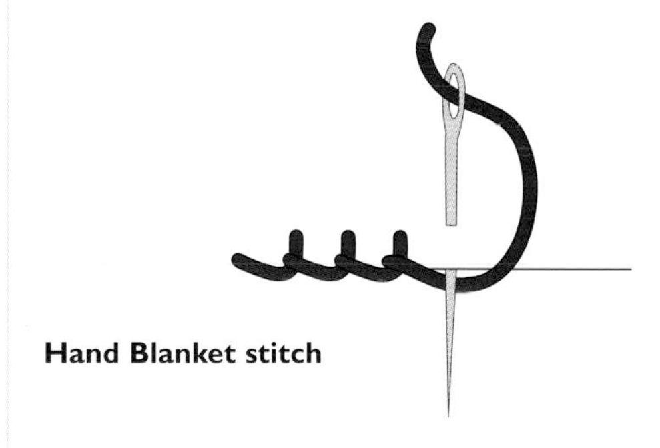

Hand Blanket stitch

Machine Appliqué

Choose a decorative stitch on your sewing machine (such as a Blanket stitch or Feather stitch) to stitch around the appliquéd shape.

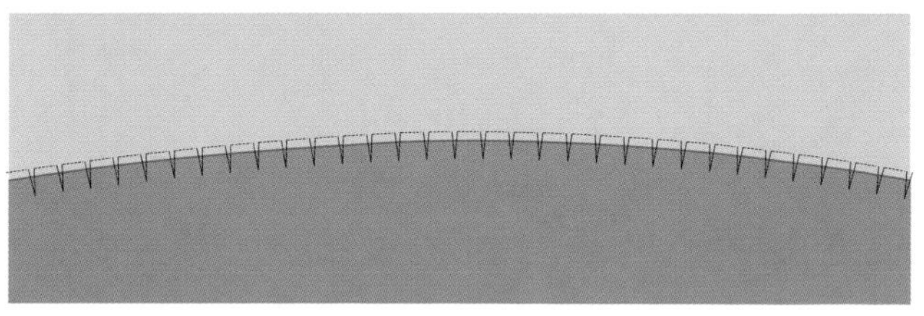

Machine Blanket stitch

Making Curved Stems

To make 1/2" wide finished stems:

1. Use 2" strips of fabric which has been cut on the bias. To make bias cut strips, fold an 18" x 22" piece of fabric.

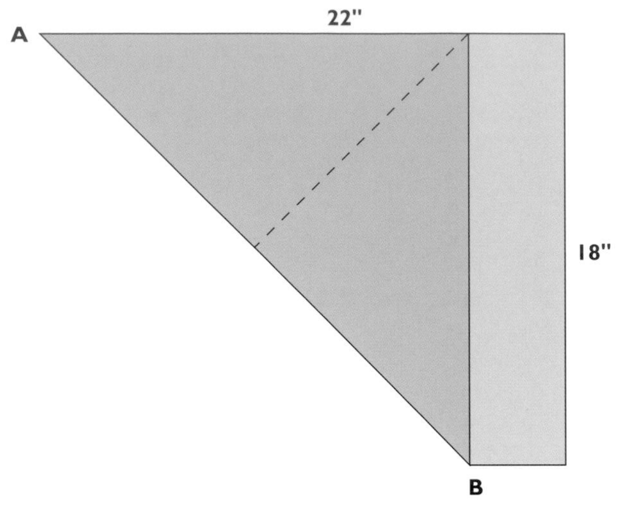

2. Fold the fabric to bring point B even with point A. There are four thicknesses along the folded edge.

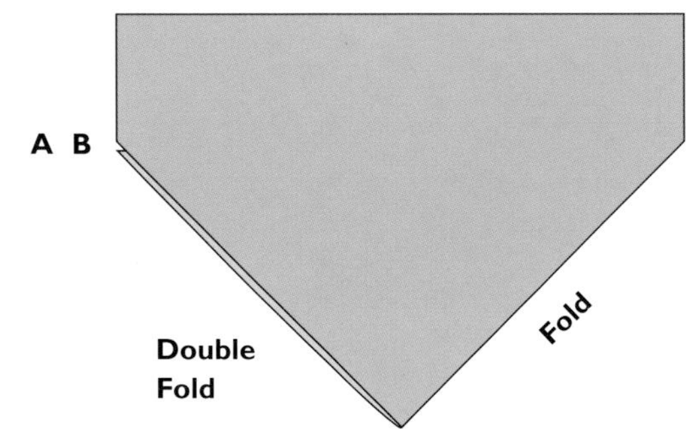

3. Rotate fabric as shown. Use the cutting tools to remove the folds on the left side. Cut a 2" strip.

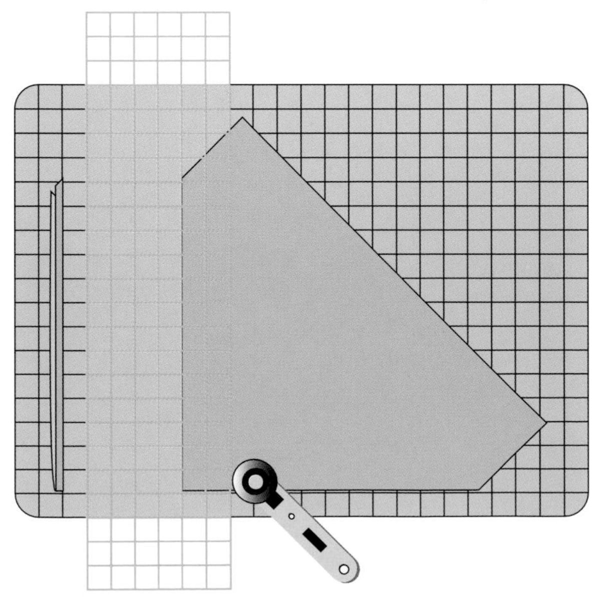

4. With the right side of the fabric facing out, fold and press a strip of fabric in half lengthwise. Then stitch 1/8" from the raw edges along the length of the strip.

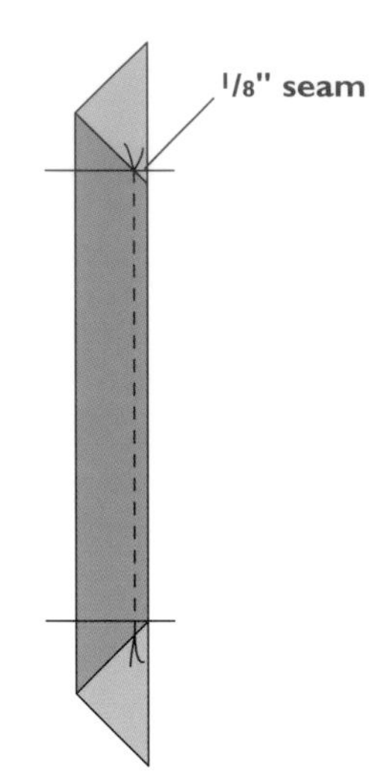

5. The strip is ready to be sewn onto the background fabric. To do this, pin the strip into the desired position and stitch 1/4" from the raw edges. Press the folded edge over the seam allowance. Then stitch the folded edge to the background fabric, either by hand or by machine.

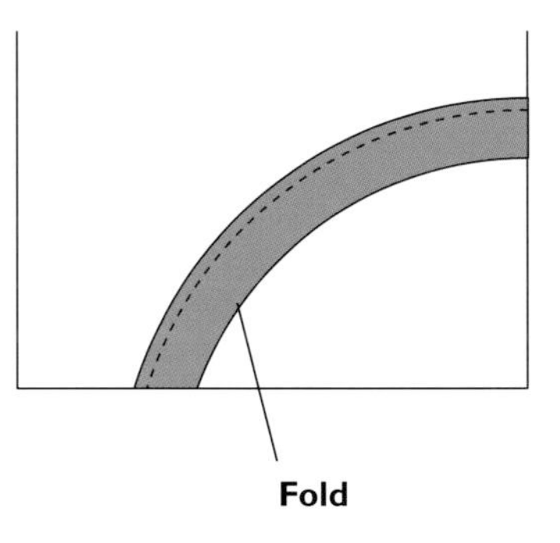

Putting it All Together

Before you begin sewing your blocks together in the desired arrangement (called setting), give your blocks a final press, using spray sizing or starch, if desired. Use your cutting tools to trim and straighten any uneven edges of the blocks. Be careful that you do not cut too much or you will lose the seam allowance.

NOTE

A design wall is useful to lay out your blocks in the desired order. A design wall is a wall or large board that is covered with a material such as batting or flannel. The material helps the blocks stay in place without pins, yet makes it easy to move blocks and pieces around for different positions within the quilt, different sets, sewing order, etc.

Sewing Blocks Together in a Straight Setting

HELPFUL HINT

Pin a piece of paper indicating the row number, to the first block of each vertical row.

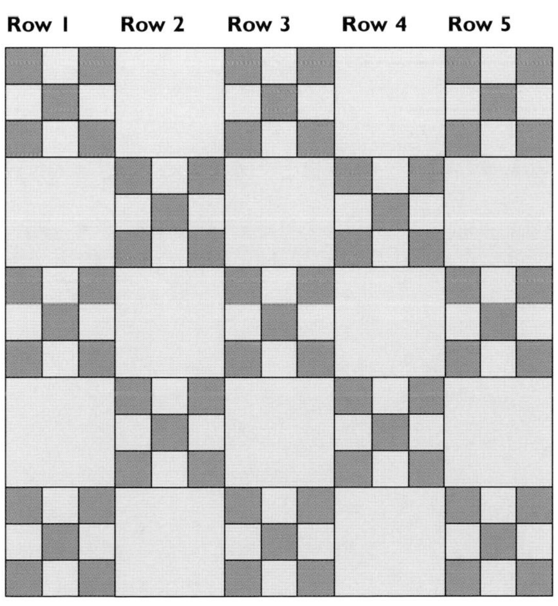

Straight setting

1. Place the top block from Row 2 right sides together with the top block from Row 1. Stitch the blocks together along their right hand edges.

2. Continue the chain of thread and sew the second set of blocks in Rows 1 and 2 together along their right-hand edges.

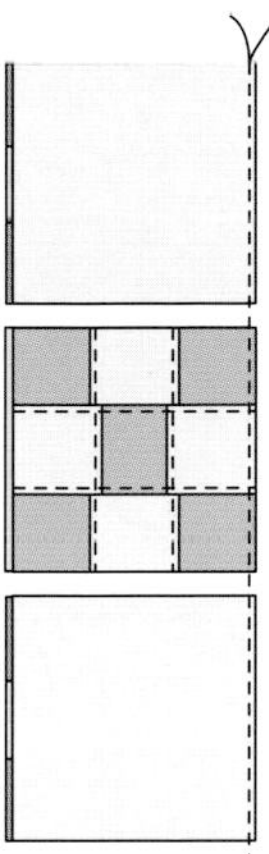

3. Continue chaining the remaining pairs of blocks from Rows 1 and 2 together in the same manner. Do not cut the chain of thread holding the pairs.

4. Next, place the first block from Row 3, right sides together, on top of the first block in Row 2. Then stitch them together along their right-hand sides. Using the same method of chaining, continue sewing the blocks from Row 3 onto the blocks in Row 2.

5. Repeat this procedure for the remaining vertical rows.

6. Press the new seams in each horizontal row in alternating directions, as shown, to prevent bulk when you join the rows.

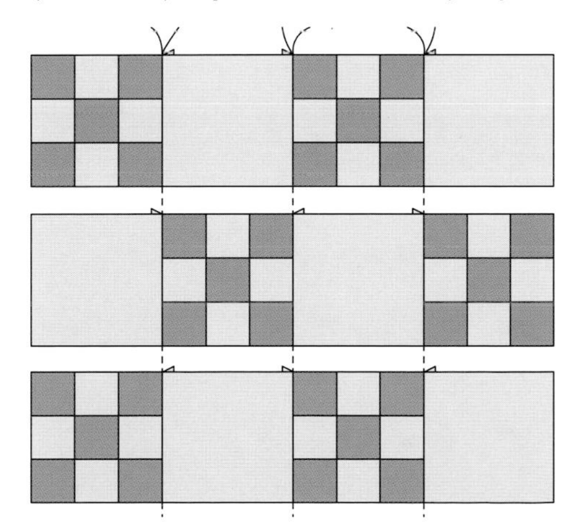

7. Sew the horizontal rows together, placing pins at the intersections of the seams.

8. Press the new seams in one direction.

9. Give the quilt top a final press first on the wrong, then the right side.

Sewing Blocks Together in a Diagonal Setting

Side and corner triangle pieces are required to complete the edges of a quilt with blocks sewn together in a diagonal setting (also called "on point").

Helpful Hint

Mark the number of each row onto a piece of paper and pin it to the first block of each row to eliminate any mix-up.

Side and corner triangles (setting triangles) should be cut larger than needed to allow for straightening the edges of the quilt top.

1. Sew the side triangles to opposite sides of the block in Row 1, as shown. Press the seams in the direction of the side triangles.

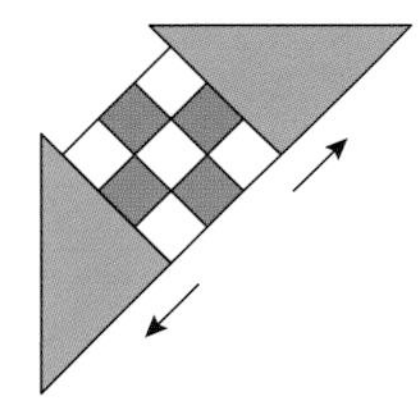

2. Sew together the side triangles and the blocks in Row 2. Press the seams in the direction opposite from those in Row 1.

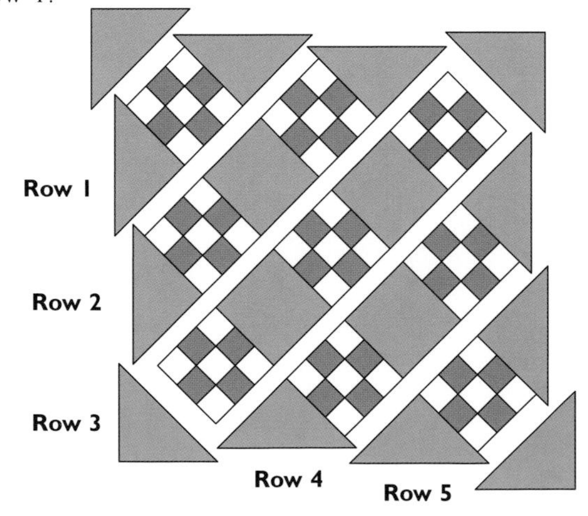

3. Sew together the blocks and side triangles in the remaining rows in the same manner.

4. Join Row 1 to Row 2, alternating the direction of the seam allowances and placing pins at the seam intersections to hold them secure.

5. Sew together the remaining rows in the same manner. Then sew on the four corner triangles.

6. Give the quilt top a final press first on the wrong, then right side. Use the cutting tools to straighten the edges and remove any excess fabric 3/8" – 1/2" beyond the corners of the blocks.

Helpful Hint

A square ruler placed on the corners of the quilt top is very helpful to square up the corners accurately.

Measuring, Cutting, and Attaching Borders

Adding Borders to Your Quilt

If you plan to add a border(s) to your quilt top, it is important to accurately determine the length of the border strips.

Note

Do not simply sew the border strips to the quilt top without first measuring. If you do, you could have rippled edges.

1. Lay the quilt top on a flat surface and use a plastic or metal tape measure to determine the measurement along both sides as well as through the center of the quilt top, as shown. Use the average of the three measurements for the cut length of the side borders.

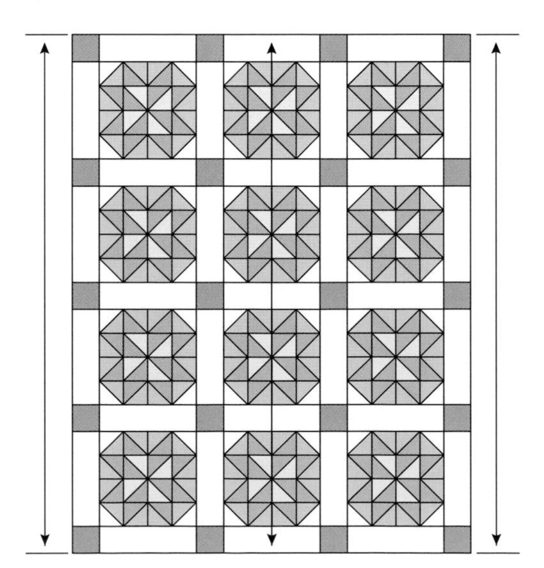

2. Place pins at the center points of the border strips and also at the center points along the corresponding sides of the quilt top, as shown.

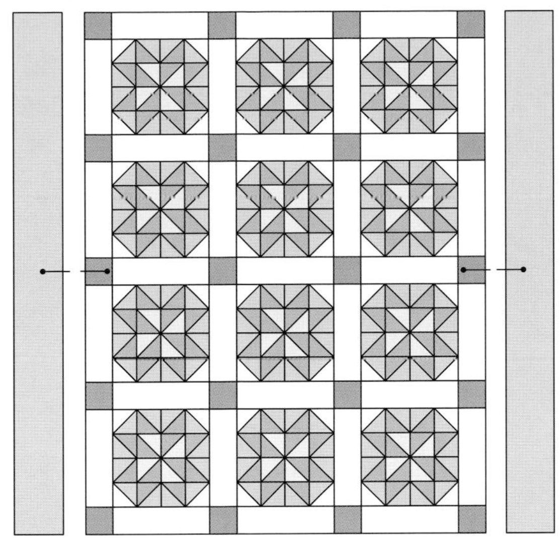

3. Lay the border strips right sides together with the quilt top, matching pins at the center points and placing pins at opposite ends to hold secure. Place additional pins along the length evenly distributing any fullness if necessary.

4. Sew with the border strips on top, since they are more stable than the quilt top and less likely to stretch.

5. Press the border strip seams first on the wrong side. Then fold the strips over the stitching line and press.

6. Lay the quilt top on a flat surface. To determine the length of the border strips for the remaining two sides of the quilt, measure both the top and the bottom, as well as through the center, as shown. Take an average of these measurements.

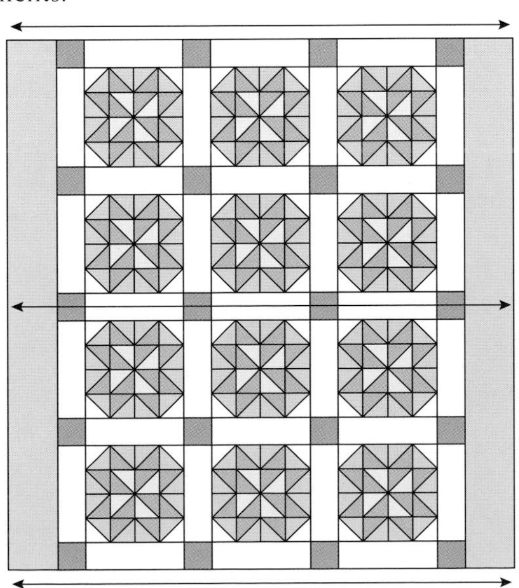

7. Place pins at the center points of these border strips and the quilt top. Then sew these strips, using the same method described for the side borders.

Backing

The fabric on the back side of your quilt (called backing) can be one piece of fabric or several fabrics sewn together. Leftover pieces of fabric can be sewn together and even extra blocks can be incorporated into the backing. It is always fun to turn a quilt to its "wrong" side and be surprised by the backing. If your backing is pieced, press any seams to one side. Do not press the seams open. The backing fabric should be at least 2" larger all the way around than the quilt top. Remember to remove the selvage edges as they are tightly woven and difficult to quilt through.

Piecing Diagrams

The following piecing diagrams were used to determine the required backing fabric for each project shown in this book.

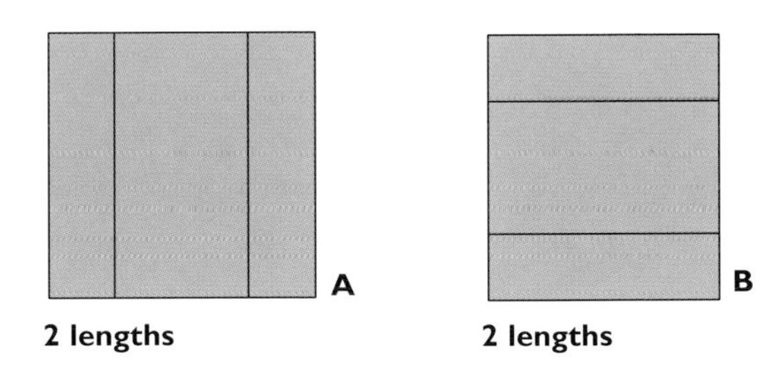

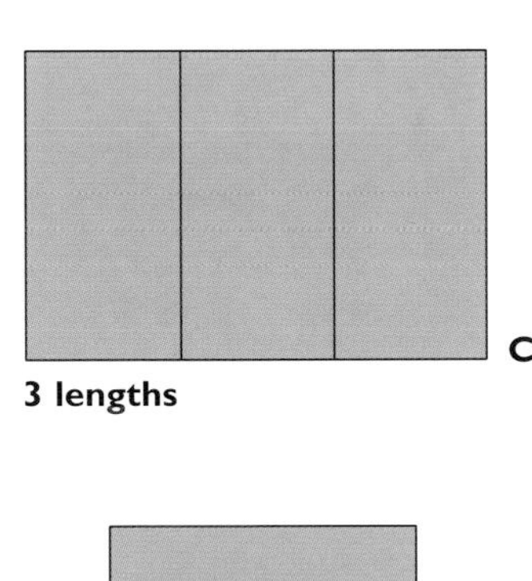

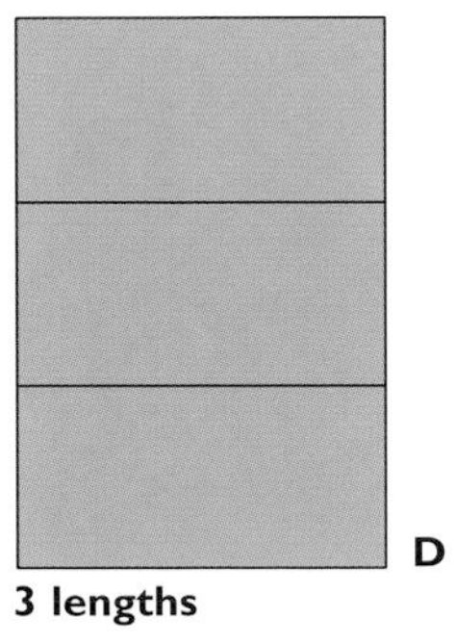

Batting

The batting is the layer between the quilt top and the backing. Choose a good quality batting which is not too lofty (thick) for your choice of quilting. Batting that is too lofty is more difficult to quilt through.

HELPFUL HINT

If using pre-packaged batting remove it from the bag and allow it to relax on a flat surface to remove any deep creases before layering and basting.

Layering and Basting

Use a large utility table (or tables) or the floor to secure the three layers (quilt top, batting, and backing) in preparation for quilting.

NOTE

If you will be hand quilting in a frame, you may be able to skip this process and proceed directly to the quilting. Just follow the manufacturer's instructions that accompany your frame. If you will be using a hoop, proceed as follows:

Basting for Hand Quilting

Supplies: Paper scissors, masking tape, straight pins, darning needle, and light colored thread (quilting thread works well).

1. With the wrong side facing up, lay the backing on the table or floor. Secure around the edges with masking tape. Tape one side and then the opposite, then tape the two remaining sides. Be sure that the backing is held taut.

HELPFUL HINT

If the direction of the backing fabric is important, take note of that as you layer the batting and top onto the backing.

2. Lay the batting on top of the backing. Smooth out any folds or creases. Use paper scissors to trim any excess batting beyond the edges of the backing. With the right side facing you, center the quilt top over the batting. Carefully smooth it flat.

3. Starting in the center of the quilt top and working out toward the edges, use straight pins to secure all three layers, placing pins approximately 6" apart.

4. Thread a darning needle with approximately 4 feet of light-colored thread. Secure one end with a knot.

5. Starting from the center of the quilt and working toward the edges, stitch the layers together with 2" diagonal basting stitches, as shown.

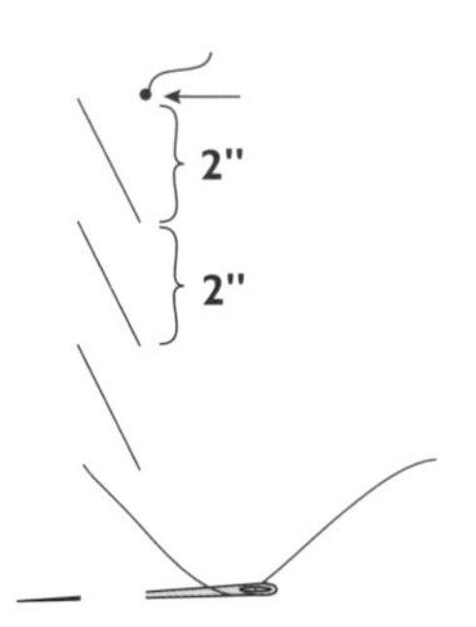

Diagonal basting stitch

6. The stitches should form a grid approximately 6" apart.

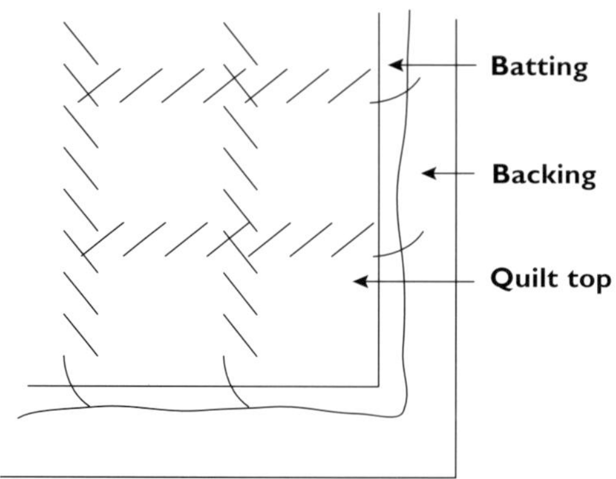

Basting in a 6" grid

7. Remove the pins and masking tape. Trim the batting to within ½" of the quilt top.

8. Fold the backing extension over the edges of the quilt top and stitch with a long running basting stitch. This will protect the edges while hand-quilting. This is **not** the finished edge of the quilt. A separate binding will be attached when the quilting is done.

Quilting

Hand Quilting

Supplies: Quilting needles (Betweens No. 8 or 9), quilting thread, finger cot, thimble, small scissors, quilting hoop

1. Thread your small Betweens needle with quilting thread (approximately 18" long), which has a knot in one end.
2. Place a thimble on the center finger of your quilting hand and a finger cot on the pointer finger of the same hand.

Helpful Hint

Finger cots are useful as grabbers for pulling the needle and thread through the three layers.

3. Insert the needle and thread, through only the top and the batting layers, and come up at the point where you want to start quilting. Then gently tug on the thread to pop the knot below the surface of the quilt top and into the batting layer.
4. Take a small backstitch. Then place the tip of the center finger of your free hand on the backside of the quilt, directly under the area to be quilted.
5. Insert the tip of the needle straight down into the quilt and push through with your thimble. As soon as the tip of the needle touches your finger, immediately bring the tip of the needle up to the front side. To do this, position the thumb of your quilting hand approximately 1" ahead of the point where the needle is inserted. Then pressing your thumb against the quilt and pushing the needle at an upward angle with your thimble finger, push the tip of the needle up. As soon as the tip of the needle is visible, insert it again through all layers, just a little ahead of where it came up. Continue with this "up-and-down" rocking motion until there are about four stitches on the tip of your needle. Then using the thimble finger, push the needle and thread all the way through, using the finger cot for assistance in pulling. Continue stitching along the marked quilting design.
6. To end the thread, take a small backstitch through the top layer only. Pull the needle and thread to the top side. Wrap the thread around the needle twice. While holding the wraps with your free hand, pull the needle through. This will create a French knot close to the surface of the quilt. At the point where the thread emerged, insert the needle into the batting layer and gently tug to pop the knot below the surface of the quilt top. Bring the needle and thread out about 1/2" away, and cut the thread.

Basting for Machine Quilting

Supplies: Paper scissors, masking tape, size 0 brass safety pins.

1. Follow Steps 1-3 for Basting for Hand Quilting, then use safety pins to secure all three layers. Place pins approximately 4"-5" apart. Avoid placing pins directly over seams or areas that will be quilted.
2. Trim the batting and backing to within 1" of the top.

Machine Quilting

Supplies: Walking foot (for straight lines and gentle curves) or darning foot (for free motion), thread (use the same weight and color in both the top and bobbin), rubber finger tips or gloves with rubber tips (can be helpful for guiding the quilt through the machine).

1. Starting in the center of one side, stitch along the seam lines first (called quilting in the ditch), in both directions.
2. Stitch motifs or patterns within the spaces. If these lines are straight or gentle curves you can use the walking foot. Otherwise, use the darning foot. When using the darning foot you must drop the feed dogs on your machine. This allows you to control the direction of the stitching and the stitch length. It takes practice to achieve a consistent and even stitch length when using a darning foot.

Helpful Hint

Work on a practice piece of fabric layered with batting and backing before attempting to quilt on your project. Start with some straight line quilting and then play with some interesting patterns, as shown. For more machine quilting ideas and techniques read *Show Me How to Machine Quilt; A Fun, No-Mark Approach* by Kathy Sandbach. Kathy quilted many of the quilts in this book.

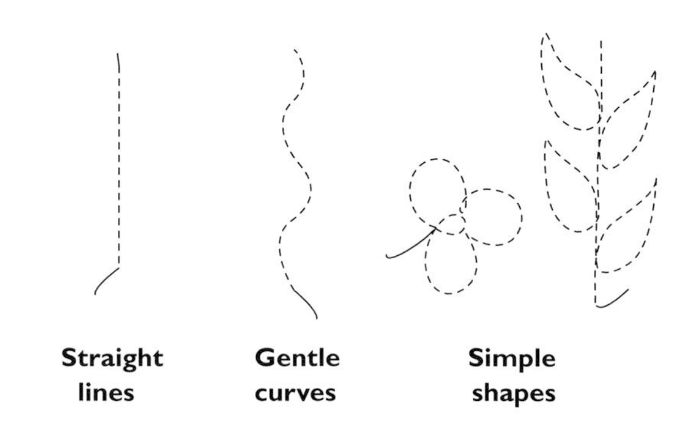

Preparation for Attaching Sleeve and Binding

1. If the backing has been basted over the edge of the quilt top remove the basting. Use a longer stitch length on your sewing machine to stitch 1/8" from the edge of the quilt top, stitching through all layers, all the way around.

Helpful Hint

A walking foot will allow the layers to feed evenly while stitching around the edge of the quilt top.

2. Use your cutting tools to remove the excess batting and backing beyond the edge of the quilt. The quilt is now ready to attach the binding and optional sleeve.

Helpful Hint

If your finished binding will be more than 1/4" wide, leave a small extension of batting and backing to fill in the space.

Making and Attaching a Sleeve

A sleeve is a tube of fabric that is sewn across the top of the quilt on the back side. It is used if you want to hang your quilt.

1. Cut a strip of fabric 6"-8" wide (leftover pieces of backing work well). The length of the strip is determined by the width of your quilt.

2. Finish the short sides of the strip by folding in the raw edges on each end, pressing them, and then stitching to make a narrow hem at each end.

3. With the right side facing out, press the strip in half lengthwise. Place the raw edges of the sleeve on the back side even with the top edge of the quilt. Attach the sleeve, stitching over the same 1/8" line which was used to hold the three layers together.

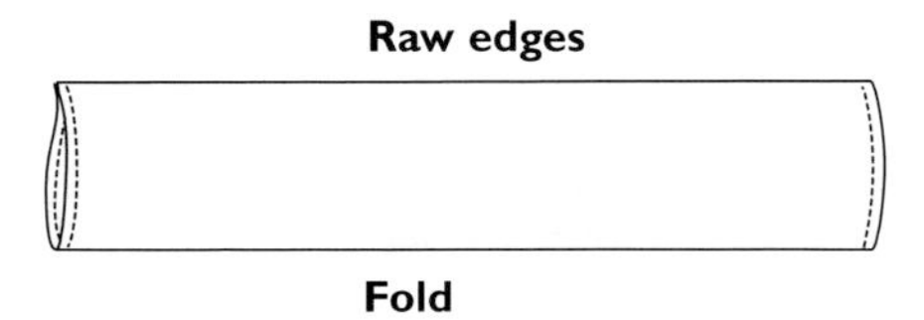

4. Use a needle and thread to hand stitch the folded edge of the sleeve to the backing, being careful to catch only the backing fabric, not the batting and quilt top. Do not stitch the sleeve ends closed.

Making and Attaching a Continuous Binding

Binding is a separate strip of fabric, which encases the raw edges of the three layers and finishes the quilt. The continuous binding forms a miter at the corners on both the front and back sides of the quilt.

1. For 1/4" wide finished binding, cut 1 7/8" strips of fabric.

2. Sew enough strips together to extend around the entire edge of the quilt plus at least 12" for turning the corners and overlapping the ends.

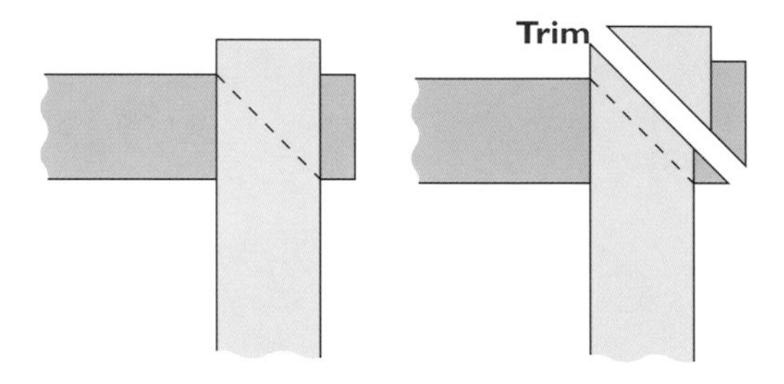

Join strip ends together with a diagonal seam.

3. Fold the starting end of the binding strip at a 45° angle, as shown. With the right side facing out, fold the binding strip in half lengthwise and press. Apply spray sizing or starch to give stability and set the crease.

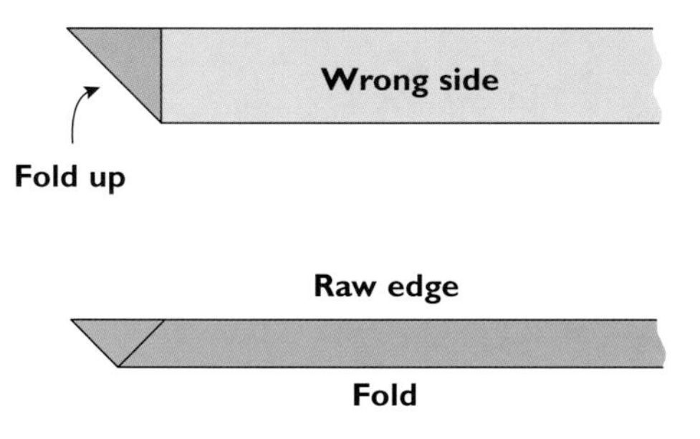

4. With the right sides together and raw edges even, lay the binding strip on the front side of the quilt.

Helpful Hint

Avoid placing a binding strip seam at a corner. Make a trial run with the binding strip around the outer edges of the quilt to determine an appropriate starting point.

Helpful Hint

A walking foot on your sewing machine is helpful in maintaining even tension while attaching the binding.

5. Starting 3" from the beginning of the binding strip, sew the binding to the quilt ¼" from the edge of the quilt top, as shown

6. Continue stitching to within ¼" of the corner. Then stop and backstitch. Remove the quilt from the machine.

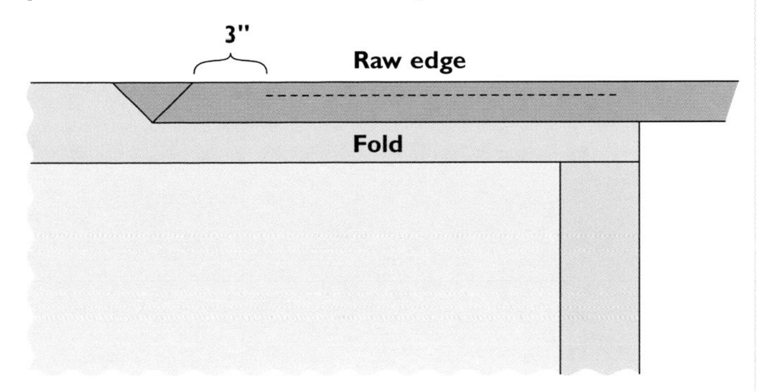

7. Lay the corner of the quilt on a flat surface and fold the binding strip away from the quilt, as shown.

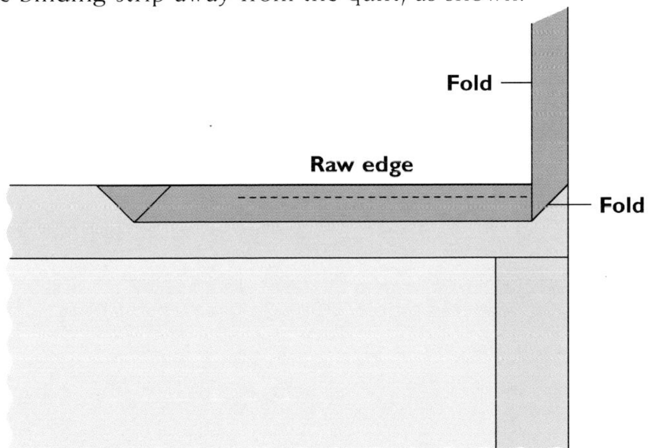

8. Fold the binding strip toward you, the top folded edge even with the top edge of the quilt top, and the raw edges even with the right-hand side of the quilt, as shown.

9. Starting at the top folded edge of the binding strip, stitch along the length to within ¼" of the next corner. Stop and backstitch.

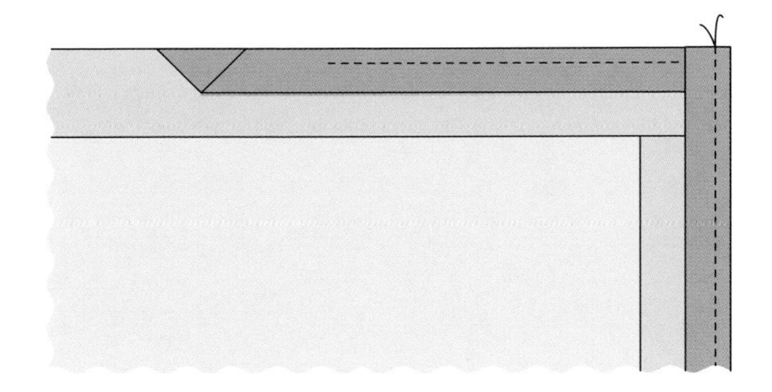

10. Remove the quilt from the machine. Repeat Steps 7–9 for the remaining sides and corners.

11. When you have sewn the binding to within 8" of the starting point, stop, backstitch, and remove the quilt from the machine. Slip the end of the binding strip into the starting end. Trim any excess length if necessary. Pin to secure. Stitch the final section of the binding to the quilt.

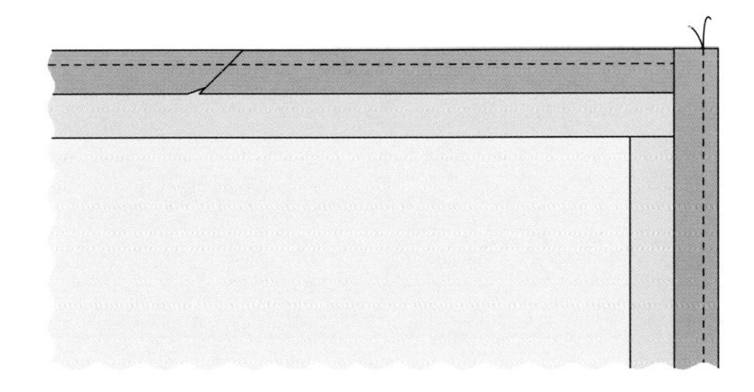

12. Turn the binding strip up and over the edge of the quilt to the back, folding the binding at the corners to form miters on both the front and back. Pin to hold the folded edge in place on the back. Use a hand slipstitch to secure the folded edge of the binding to the backing, being careful to catch only the backing fabric.

Appliqué Patterns

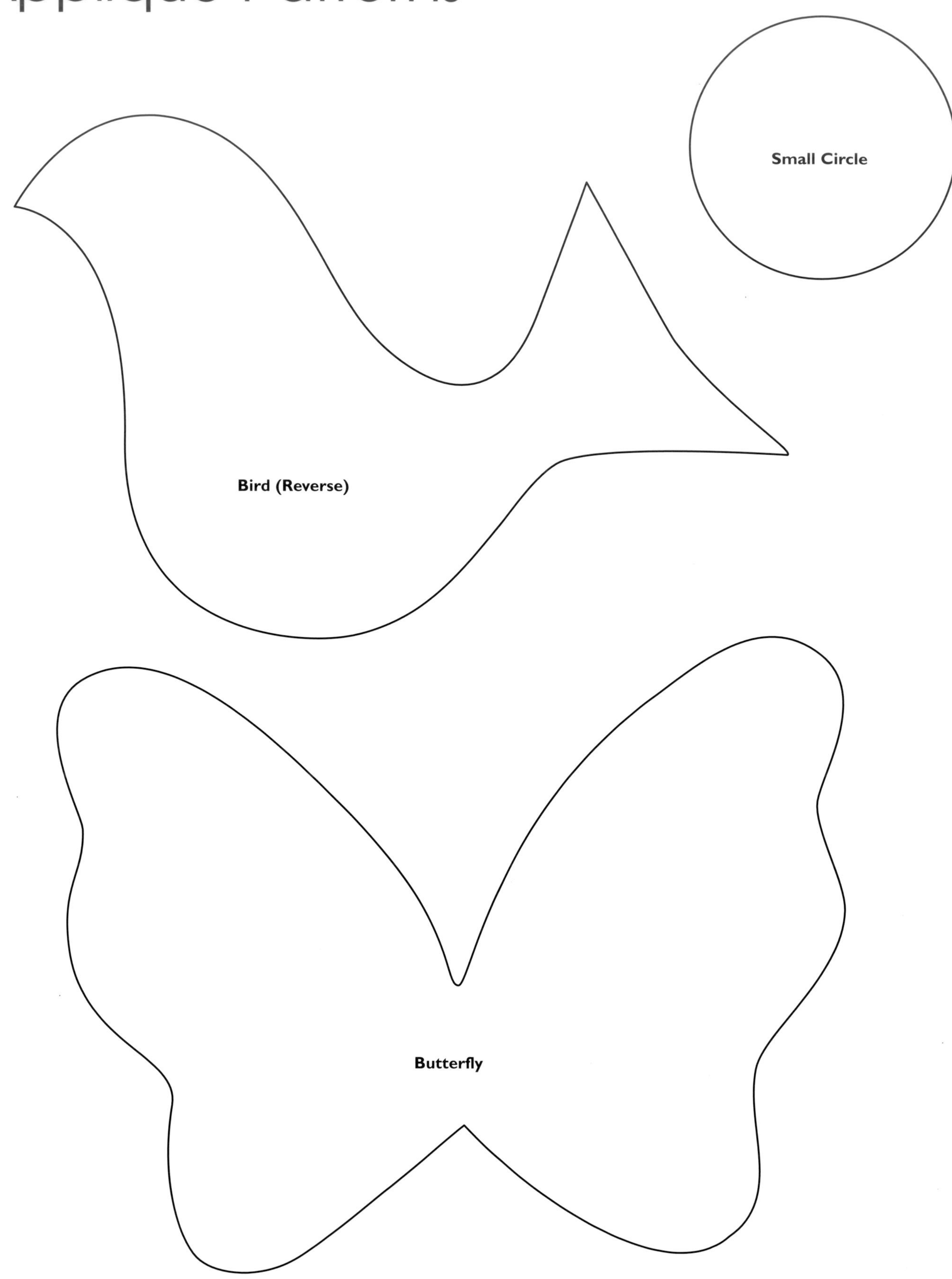

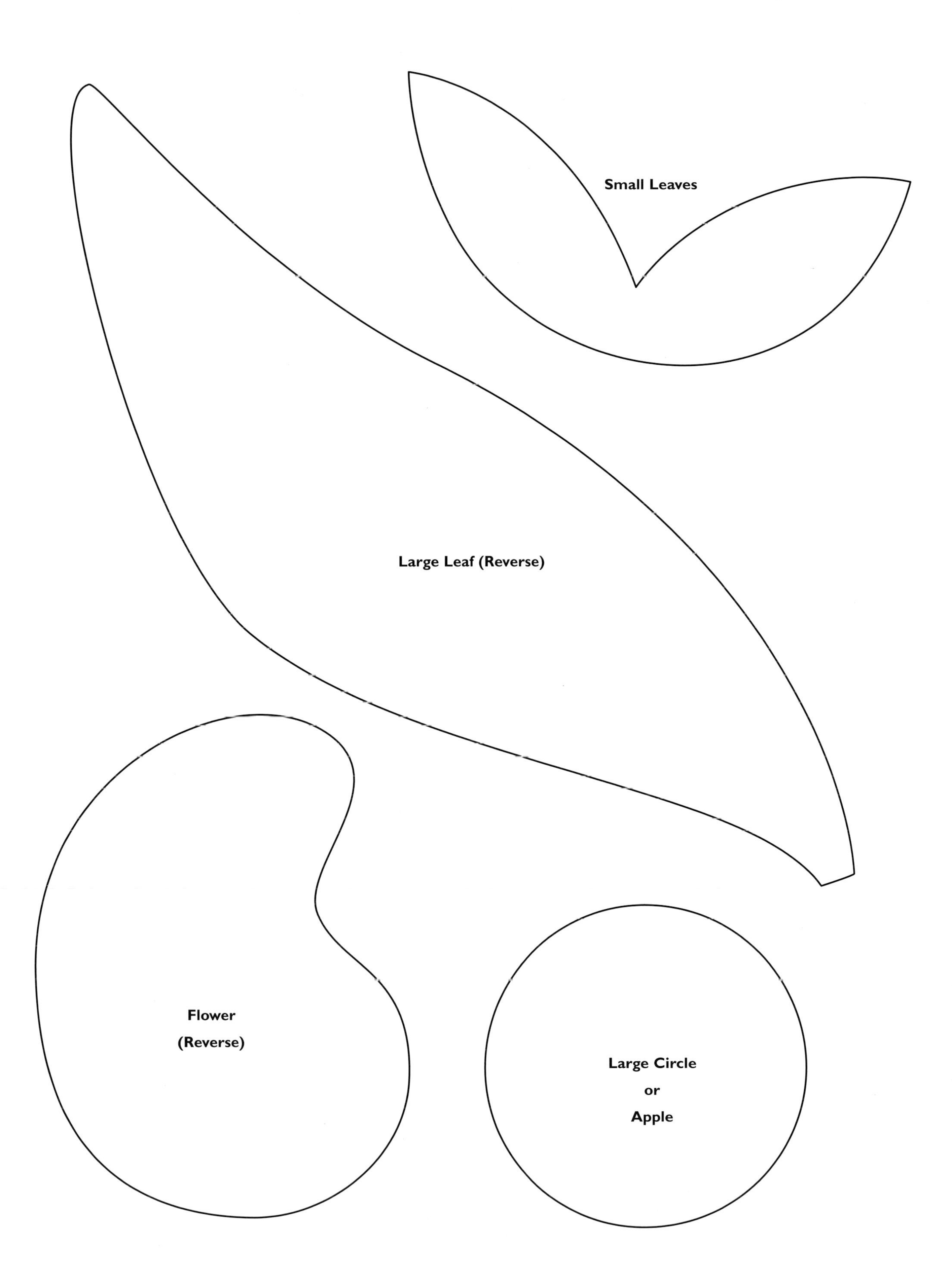
Small Leaves
Large Leaf (Reverse)
Flower
(Reverse)
Large Circle
or
Apple

Class Outline for Teachers

CLASS ONE:

Parts of A Quilt – page 9

Planning, Supplies & Equipment, Fabric Selection – pages 9-12

Techniques: Quick-Cutting and Strip Piecing – pages 95-98

Demonstrations: Nine-Patches (make seven) and Fence (make one set) – pages 14-17

CLASS TWO:

Techniques: Half-Square Triangles and Quarter-Square Triangles – pages 27, 42

Demonstrations: Half-Square Triangles (nine) and Birdhouse (make two) – pages 27, 44

CLASS THREE:

Techniques: More Quick-Cutting

Demonstrations:

Square-in-a-Square (make five) and Basket (make two from one Square-in-a-Square block) – pages 48, 51

CLASS FOUR:

Techniques: More Quick-Cutting and Appliqué

Demonstrations: House (make one) and Appliquéd Bird, Apples, and Leaves – pages 63, 98

CLASS FIVE:

Putting it All Together – page 101

CLASS SIX:

Layering and Basting – page 104

CLASS SEVEN:

Demonstrations:

Quilting and Binding – pages 104-107

About The Authors

Diana McClun's career as a quiltmaker blossomed in mid-life, inspired by her mother and grandmother's fascination with fabric and quilts. As a toddler playing in her mother's kitchen Diana recalls playing with fabric scraps kept visibly in the flour bin to amuse her while her mother worked.

With a college Wool Growers and 4-H scholarship Diana found the University of Idaho the place to study clothing and textiles. As her passion for and understanding of fiber blossomed, her attention turned to making an original wedding dress as a class project. A trousseau followed, as did the joy of learning from others as many joined in the creation of eight handmade quilts for the bride-to-be. She now has a five generation legacy of quiltmaking after she taught several grandchildren how to quilt.

In 1970 she enrolled at San Jose State University to pursue studies in fine arts. Eventually her love of fabric lead her to San Francisco State University and the further study of textiles.

By 1980 Diana was ready to abandon the teaching of tailored garments and pursue a dream working in the creative art of quiltmaking. With her training in education, art and textiles she operated a business (Empty Spools) in Alamo, CA centered around fabrics and quiltmaking but with an emphasis on classroom teaching.

It was during this time college graduate Laura Nownes was seeking a new kind of employment utilizing her artistic gifts. Laura became a quiltmaking instructor and store manager. Laura's passion for making quilts is an extension of her love of sewing. From an early age she began with doll clothes, then to making her own garments and often working on projects for neighbors. Her early involvement in 4-H provided her first teaching experience to younger members. After taking her first sampler quilt class in 1979, she knew she had found a lifelong interest. Her connection with Diana in 1980 allowed her to share her talents with students in the classroom. Laura soon became one of the shop's leading beginning quilting teachers. It was then Diana and Laura began the friendship which has led to the creation of five landmark quiltmaking books and a text for beginning and intermediate quiltmaking.

In 1986 while Laura was on maternity leave with her first daughter, Diana approached her about co-authoring a beginning how-to book. The book was intended to be used just in the shop. However, it was chosen by local publisher Michael Kile of The Quilt Digest Press. Shortly thereafter, *Quilts! Quilts!! Quilts!!!* was born. The huge, immediate success of this book encouraged Diana and Laura to continue writing.

The pair has worked together on television programs, with study groups, and in seminars touching thousands of students, giving them a start in the basics of quiltmaking. They founded Teacher Development Seminars as a result of their commitment to the continuing education of quiltmaking. They facilitate the annual C&T Publishing Teachers Retreat which is another avenue for training those interested in learning the skills of teaching and quiltmaking with classes taught by well-known quilting authors.

For the past 17 years Diana has been co-founder and director of Empty Spools Seminars, held at Asilomar Conference Center in Pacific Grove, CA. With four seminars per year, one thousand students are taught by forty-five of the nation's best instructors during these five-day seminars.

Index

All quilts in bold *italics* are projects.